WHAT DOES *the* FUTURE HOLD?

Haven ministries
sent this book to me.

WHAT DOES *the* FUTURE HOLD?

EXPLORING VARIOUS VIEWS ON THE END TIMES

C. MARVIN PATE

BakerBooks

a division of Baker Publishing Group
Grand Rapids, Michigan

Published by Baker Books
a division of Baker Publishing Group
P.O. Box 6287, Grand Rapids, MI 49516-6287
www.bakerbooks.com

Printed in the United States of America

Library of Congress Cataloging-in-Publication Data
Pate, C. Marvin, 1952–
    What does the future hold? : exploring various views on the end times /
C. Marvin Pate.
        p.   cm.
    Includes bibliographical references (p.   ).
    ISBN 978-0-8010-7204-8 (pbk.)
        1. Millennialism. 2. Millennium (Eschatology). 3. End of the world. 4. Eschatology. I. Title.
BT892.P38 2010
236'.9—dc22   2009037686

10   11   12   13   14   15   16   7   6   5   4   3   2   1

Contents

Introduction

Prophecy at a Fever Pitch

The end of the world is near! Or so it seems. Take May 17, 2008, for example. In the course of a mere twenty-four hours, the network and cable news programs announced in rapid-fire fashion that the death toll from the cyclone that hit Myanmar (which only now is recovering from the earlier tsunami) numbered upwards of fifty thousand people; the earthquake that rocked China has already crushed the lives of thousands; a terrorist bomb killed eighty in India (which is but an echo of Al Qaeda's attacks in Iraq); Israel plans to bomb Iran before it nukes Palestine; the war in Iraq with its cost in lives and treasure has brought President Bush's favorable ratings to an all-time low of 20 percent (this while the price of gas surpasses four dollars a gallon); cancer, aids, hunger, heart attacks, strokes, violence, drugs, along with the economy, the weather, and the environmental crisis are all out of control! Besides these news briefs, it is obvious that the American middle class is shrinking; the dollar is plummeting; the oil companies are making a killing; the U.S. military is stretched too thin; the 2008 national election has polarized the country along racial lines; (and evangelical Christianity is giving way to an amorphous, emergent church that, ironically, finds its heroes in the early Fathers of church tradition!)

All hell seems to be breaking loose! The signs of the times hailing the return of Christ and the end of the world as we know it have never been more intense. Like labor pangs, they are unleashing their fury on planet Earth. Or so it appears.

Not surprisingly, prophecy is at a fever pitch. May 2008 witnessed the sixtieth anniversary of the rebirth of the State of Israel. Indeed, that event in 1948 stirred up interest in end-time prophecy as little before it had done. For many, Jesus's prediction—"this generation will certainly not pass away until all these things have happened" (Matt. 24:34; Mark 13:30; Luke 21:32)—referred to the generation that dawned with the return of Jews to Palestine in 1948. Never mind that the date of Christ's return kept being revised from 1978 to 1988 to 1998 to 2008! Still, the conviction stands that the end is nearer than ever.

(The regathering of Israel as a nation has inspired a proliferation of prophecy) books, films, and conferences, especially works by Hal Lindsey (particularly his *Late Great Planet Earth*) and the Left Behind series. These publications alone have sold millions and millions of copies, thereby inspiring a whole generation of prophecy buffs who feverishly attempt to match contemporary events with biblical predictions about the end times. Pursuing this angle toward Revelation, the last book in the Bible, these interpreters equate Red China with the "kings from the East" (Rev. 16:12–16), the European Common Market with the "ten horns" of the beast (13:1–10), the mark of the beast (666) of Revelation 13 with everything from credit cards to the Internet, and the Antichrist with a parade of prominent people, including Adolf Hitler, Benito Mussolini, Henry Kissinger, and Mikhail Gorbachev. This intense fascination with Revelation by the doomsayers shows no sign of decreasing in the twenty-first century.

But Christianity does not have a monopoly on predicting the end of the world: Nostradamus (who died in 1566) forecast that the millennium (Latin for one thousand years of peace and bliss on earth) would arrive in 2026. Michael Drosnin's *Bible Code I* and *II* predicted that World War III would occur in 2006. The Mayans prophesy that the end of the world will be in 2012. Zoroastrianism, which has its roots in Persian (Iranian) soil, expects at any time the end-time holy war to break out. According to Islamic extremists like Mahmoud Ahmadinejad, president of Iran, this battle will be between faithful Muslims on the one hand and infidels (Jews, Christians, and all others) on the other hand.

For their part, many Hasidic Jews expect the Messiah to come and destroy the Dome of the Rock in Jerusalem, replacing it with the end-time holy temple predicted in Ezekiel 40–48. Indeed, when the late prime minister of Israel, Ariel Sharon, stepped onto the Temple Mount early in his term of office, many of his compatriots thought that the time of the end-time temple was drawing near. So did Palestinians, which is why they began the Second Intifada. The Melanesia cargo cults also eagerly await their Messiah to transfer to them all European goods and thereby topple colonial rule. And so the prophecies go.

But not so fast! Is the world really coming to an end? Or is the preceding apocalyptic portrait of life as we know it today somehow distorted? If so, what other explanations might there be for the dire shape of our planet? To put it another way: is the world getting worse or is it possible that the present situation is but the proverbial storm before the blissful calm that will soon wash over us all, in history no less? These questions broach the subject of millenarianism, the belief that a period of utopia (one thousand years?) will one day be known in the world. At that time righteousness will replace sin; healing will overtake sickness; peace will conquer war; life will swallow up death; or, as Isaiah the prophet eloquently expressed it:

"Behold, I will create new heavens and a new earth. The former things will not be remembered, nor will they come to mind. . . . Never again will there be in it an infant who lives but a few days, or an old man who does not live out his years; he who dies at a hundred will be thought a mere youth; he who fails to reach a hundred will be considered accursed. They will build houses and dwell in them; they will plant vineyards and eat their fruit. No longer will they build houses and others live in them, or plant and others eat. For as the days of a tree, so will be the days of my people; my chosen ones will long enjoy the works of their hands. They will not toil in vain or bear children doomed to misfortune; for they will be a people blessed by the LORD, they and their descendants with them. Before they call I will answer; while they are still speaking I will hear. The wolf and the lamb will feed together, and the lion will eat straw like the ox, but dust will be the serpent's food. They will neither harm nor destroy on all my holy mountain," says the LORD.

Isaiah 65:17, 20–25

Actually the hope for the millennium is nothing new. In biblical literature, the eager anticipation of the coming kingdom of God is a theme that dominates both Old and New Testaments, a vision that has sustained the church throughout the centuries. And today when we cut through the fog of war, depression/recession, and sickness, isn't that really what we long for too—the arrival of the millennium? This book answers that question with an emphatic yes!

The premillennial school emphasizes the not-yet aspect of the kingdom of God. The kingdom is already here to some extent (in connection with the first coming of Christ) but not yet in its fullness (this awaits the future second coming of Christ). It reads Revelation literally, with bulldog determination. Thus premillennialists would say, "Thy kingdom come."

The postmillennial school of thought emphasizes the already aspect of end-time prophecy (though some in this camp

10

allow for the not-yet aspect of a future return of Christ). The first coming of Christ brought the kingdom in its fullness, which heralded the gospel of the new covenant in the millennium. And in the judgment of Jerusalem in AD 70, Christ came again. This view also reads Revelation literally, at least to a certain degree. Thus they would say, "Thy kingdom came."

The amillennialist school of thought balances the two other views: the kingdom already came but is not yet fully triumphant. These two time frames correspond to the first and second comings of Christ—the first in history and the second at the end of history. Thus this view sees both the kingdom and tribulation as present spiritual realities, based on its allegorical hermeneutic. Therefore, amillennialists would say, "Thy kingdom came and thy kingdom come."

A fourth view of the millennium—the skeptical interpretation—came on strong in the early twentieth century. It debunks any idea that the kingdom of God is coming or that it is the solution to the world's problems. Obviously, in orientation such a perspective is anti-Christian yet it has many followers today.

Forming bookends to the four chapters on premillennial, postmillennial, amillennial, and skeptical schools of interpretation, the opening chapter will provide a summary of the importance of end-time prophecy to the Bible, along with a brief history of millenarianism in the church, while the last chapter will offer sound principles for interpreting prophetic/apocalyptic literature in the Bible. The key biblical text on the millennium is Revelation 20:1–6. The interpretation of these verses will occupy us throughout the ensuing chapters:

> And I saw an angel coming down out of heaven, having the key to the Abyss and holding in his hand a great chain. He seized the dragon, that ancient serpent, who is the devil, or Satan, and bound him for a thousand years. He threw him into the abyss, and locked and sealed it over him to keep

him from deceiving the nations anymore until the thousand years were ended. After that, he must be set free for a short time. I saw thrones on which were seated those who had been given authority to judge. And I saw the souls of those who had been beheaded because of their testimony for Jesus and because of the word of God. They had not worshiped the beast or his image and had not received his mark on their foreheads or their hands. They came to life and reigned with Christ a thousand years. (The rest of the dead did not come to life until the thousand years were ended.) This is the first resurrection. Blessed and holy are those who have part in the first resurrection. The second death has no power over them, but they will be priests of God and of Christ and will reign with him for a thousand years.

Revelation 20:1–6

1

A Brief History of Prophecy

How the Church Has Viewed the End of the World

The pope celebrated Mass on New Year's Eve, which was to usher in the end of history. Crowds thronged the square of St. Peter's Basilica. Thousands gathered in Jerusalem awaiting Jesus's return. And in Europe, myriads awaiting the final tick of the clock of history donated land, homes, and goods to the poor in acts of contrition.

At last the clock in St. Peter's Basilica struck twelve—and nothing happened. No return of Christ, no end of history, no fire from heaven.

Was the preceding alarm about the end of the world[1] written recently? No. Actually it was a failed prediction that the world was about to end before the clock struck AD 1000. Interestingly enough, predictions about the end of the world in AD 999 remind one of similar forecasts in 1999, fueled by Y2K panic (that at midnight on December 31, 1999, millions of computers throughout the world would crash, setting the stage for a coming world government prophesied in Revelation).

This chapter looks at the phenomenon of biblical prophecy and how the church has understood that dynamic throughout its history. We begin with a not-so-good example of how to interpret biblical prophecy—William Miller's two predictions about the date of the return of Christ. These failed predictions stem from not grasping the already/not-yet aspects of biblical prophecy.

"The Great Disappointment"

Perhaps the most famous failed predictions about the end of the world were the dates William Miller set for the return of Christ. A Baptist minister, William Miller (1782–1849) founded Seventh Day Adventism and predicted that Jesus would return in about 1843. Miller's theory for coming to such a conclusion was quite elaborate, but central to it was his interpretation of two verses in the book of Daniel, which he tied together to calculate the Lord's return—Daniel 8:14, "And he said to him, 'For two thousand and three hundred evenings and mornings; then the sanctuary shall be restored'" (KJV); and Daniel 9:24, "Seventy weeks of years are decreed concerning your people and your holy city, to finish the transgression, to put an end to sin, and to atone for iniquity, to bring in everlasting righteousness, to seal both vision and prophet, and to anoint a most Holy place" (KJV). Miller's basic reasoning can be outlined as follows:

1. The sanctuary cleansing mentioned in Daniel 8:14 referred to the return of Christ, which would eradicate all evil on the earth.
2. A prophetic day equaled one year, so one could correctly calculate the numbers in the passages as 2,300 years and 490 years (seventy times seven).
3. Using Bishop Ussher's popular Old Testament chronology, the 2,300-year period began with the return of the Jews to Jerusalem to rebuild the city in 457 BC (Christ's

crucifixion, AD 33, marked the end of Daniel's seventy weeks. Moving back 490 years from AD 33, one comes to the year 457 BC).

4. Two thousand, three hundred years forward from 457 BC was AD 1843. Miller predicted that Christ would return "about" 1843. But at the beginning of 1843, Miller specifically calculated the second advent would occur between March 21, 1843, and March 21, 1844. (1. Daniel 9:24 AD 33 [Christ's death] minus 490 years equals 457 BC; 2. The Daniel 8:14 figure is 2,300 years minus 457 years equals 1843.)

Although initially Miller was reluctant to make his prediction too public, he and his followers (the Millerites) eventually set a date for the return of Christ at March 21, 1844. As that date approached, apparently many did not plant their crops that spring while others closed their stores or gave away their goods in anticipation of the event. Reportedly, a number of Millerites clothed themselves in white robes and awaited the end of the world on the hillsides of the Northeast.

When Christ failed to return on March 21, 1844, Miller and his devotees reset the date for the end of the world at October 22, 1844. When Christ did not return then, the "Great Disappointment" ensued. Some abandoned the notion of a second coming. Others went on to hold tighter yet to an imminent return of Christ. This group became the Jehovah's Witnesses, which predicted that Christ would return in 1914. Still others reinterpreted the nonevent by arguing that Christ did indeed return, but it was in heaven, where he cleansed the heavenly sanctuary. This "sanctuary doctrine" became the hallmark of the Seventh-day Adventist movement, which exists today.

Understanding End-Time Events

But how can we today avoid such prophecy gone awry? How should we interpret the Bible in the matter of end-time events?

15

We do well to start by understanding the importance of biblical prophecy in general and the kingdom of God in particular. These topics provide our next two points.

The Importance of Biblical Prophecy

While not all prophecy in the Bible deals with the future (some, perhaps much of it, is God's Word for the prophet's present day), a good portion of biblical prophecy is predictive. Note the following statistics.

THE BIBLE AND PREDICTIONS

Amount of predictive matter in the Bible: 8,352 verses, out of its total of 31,124

Proportion that is predictive: 27 percent; Old Testament: 28.5 percent; New Testament: 21.5 percent

Books with the most predictive material:

Old Testament

Ezekiel: 821 verses

Jeremiah: 812 verses

Isaiah: 754 verses

New Testament

Matthew: 278 verses

Revelation: 256 verses

Luke: 250 verses

Books most highly predictive according to the proportion of verses involving forecasts of the future:

Old Testament

Zephaniah: 89 percent predictive

Obadiah: 81 percent predictive

Nahum: 74 percent predictive

New Testament

Revelation: 63 percent predictive

Hebrews: 45 percent predictive

2 Peter: 41 percent predictive

Books with the most predictions in symbolical form: Revelation, 24; Daniel, 20[2]

Near and Far Fulfillments

The careful reader of the above will recognize that often biblical predictions have two types of fulfillment: a near and a far fulfillment. The near fulfillment happened not long after the prophet's prophecy. The far fulfillment came to fruition long after the death of the prophet, or it still has to be fulfilled. Three examples will show this near/far–fulfillment dynamic to be the case for biblical prophecy—two from the Old Testament and one from the New Testament. Scholars often label this dynamic "the already/not-yet" aspect of predictive prophecy.[3]

Isaiah 7:10–16

Near Fulfillment—Isaiah 7:10–16	Far Fulfillment— Matthew 1:21
Unnamed son of King Ahaz	Jesus

In the near fulfillment Isaiah spoke of God's deliverance from the Syrian/Israelite coalition against Judah in 732 BC. By then the child born of King Ahaz and the young woman (whoever she may have been in the king's harem) would have been three years old (assuming Isaiah's prophecy was uttered in 735 BC). And when Jews in the southern kingdom saw or heard about the child, they proclaimed the son to be "Immanuel," because his presence was proof that God kept his promise to Ahaz to protect his kingdom from Syria and northern Israel.

But what of Matthew 1:21? The far-fulfillment perspective sees a partial fulfillment of Isaiah 7:10–16 in God's deliverance of Judah from the Syro-Ephraimite (Israelite) coalition but believes the final, complete fulfillment of the Immanuel prophecy is rightly to be equated with Jesus, as Matthew well notes.

Daniel 9:24–27: The (rather) near fulfillment of Daniel's prophetic seventy weeks took place during the persecution of Jews by Antiochus Epiphanes from 171 to 164 BC. This ended when the Jewish freedom fighter Judas Maccabees delivered and cleansed the Jerusalem temple from its oppressors. The details of that fulfillment are summarized in chart form:

587–586 BC (beginning of Babylonian captivity) to 538 BC (Joshua the high priest)	605 BC (date of Jeremiah's prophecy) to 171 BC (murder of the high priest Onias III)	171 BC (Antiochus Epiphanes' persecution of the Jews) to 164 BC (the restoration of the temple)

The far fulfillment of Daniel 9:24–27 will be the persecution of the people of God by the Antichrist, according to Revelation 6–18; at least that's how many interpret its ultimate fulfillment.

The Olivet Discourse: Jesus's discourse (Matthew 24; Mark 13; Luke 21; cf. with Revelation 6–18) records his predictions about his second coming in judgment, which is divided into a near view and a far view. The near fulfillment took place in the form of the Romans' destruction of Jerusalem in AD 70. This serves as the backdrop to the far fulfillment—the second coming of Christ at the end of history to judge the earth. Using Matthew 24 as a guide, we chart the already (near)/not yet (far) fulfillments of Jesus's coming in judgment as follows:

The Already	The Not Yet
Partial fulfillment (Matt. 24:4–20; cf. Mark 13:5–23; Luke 21:8–24; Revelation 6)	Final fulfillment (Matt. 24:21–31; cf. Mark 13:24–27; Luke 21:25–36; Revelation 8–11; 15–18)
Tribulation (Matt. 24:8)	_Great tribulation_ (Matt. 24:21, 29)

The Already	The Not Yet
Messianic pretenders (vv. 4–5)	*Messianic pretenders* (vv. 23–26)
Wars (vv. 6–7)	*Wars* (v. 28)
Persecution (vv. 9–10)	*Persecution* (v. 22)
Apostasy (vv. 11–12)	*Apostasy* (v. 24)
Fall of Jerusalem (vv. 15–20)	*Second coming of Christ* (vv. 30–31)

The upshot of the already(near)/not-yet(far) dynamic is that some of predictive prophecy has already been fulfilled while some has not. And history helps to sort out which is which. Ultimately this is where William Miller, and many like him, went wrong: they have not distinguished between what has been fulfilled and what has yet to be fulfilled. In other words, they do not seem to be aware of the already/not-yet phenomenon of biblical prophecy. Thus, for example, Miller failed to understand that much of Daniel 8–9 was already fulfilled in the days of Antiochus Epiphanes and Judas Maccabees (171–164 BC). Likewise, many interpreters fail to realize that a good portion of the Olivet Discourse was already fulfilled at the fall of Jerusalem to the Romans in AD 70.

This near/far fulfillment dynamic is not the whole answer to the issue of biblical prophecy, but it does greatly clarify matters. This will become clear as we progress through this chapter and the book as a whole. So to restate our premise: failed interpretation of biblical prophecy stems in large part from not grasping the already/not-yet aspects of fulfilled prophecy.

The Kingdom of God

Considering the discussion above regarding predictive prophecy, we see an overarching theme that ties together the Old and New Testaments—the kingdom of God. Both Jew and Christian longed for the arrival of the kingdom of God; that is the millennium. Related to this are the terms *eschatology* and *apocalypticism*. We will explore these terms in

19

chapter 6, but for now we can say that the two are essentially synonymous. *Eschatology* refers to the end of time while *apocalypticism* is a specific genre, both biblical literature and contemporary nonbiblical material, that reveals the unfolding of the kingdom of God at the end of history. Undergirding all of this is the idea of "the last days" (Isa. 2:2; Micah 4:1; Acts 2:17; 2 Tim. 3:1; 2 Peter 3:3), "the last times" (1 Peter 1:20; Jude 18), or "the last hour" (1 John 2:18). To put it another way, the end time began with the first coming of Christ (the "already" aspect of eschatology), but the final fulfillment of the end of the world will not occur until the second coming of Christ (the "not-yet" aspect of eschatology). We now summarize how this is the case with the New Testament authors.[4]

The kingdom of God is a major theme in the Bible. Its origin is the Old Testament, where the emphasis falls on God's kingship. God is king of Israel (Exod. 15:18; Num. 23:21; Deut. 33:5; Isa. 43:15) and of all the earth (2 Kings 19:15; Ps. 29:10; 99:1–4; Isa. 6:5; Jer. 46:18). Juxtaposed with the concept of God's *present* reign as king are references to a day when God will *become* king over his people (Isa. 24:23; 33:22; 52:7; Zeph. 3:15; Zech. 14:9). This emphasis on God's kingship continues throughout Judaism and takes on special significance in Jewish apocalypticism with its anticipation of the age to come/kingdom of God, which abandoned any hope for present history. Only at the end of the age will the kingdom of God come.

The kingdom of God assumes center stage throughout the New Testament, especially in the Synoptic Gospels (Matthew, Mark, and Luke). And that is where we will put our attention for the moment. In the Synoptic Gospels alone, the term "the kingdom of God" occurs more than one hundred times (in Matthew only is "kingdom of heaven" a synonym for "kingdom of God"). The term that best describes the dynamic of the kingdom of God in the three Gospels, "inaugurated eschatology," is a concept commonly connected with the twentieth-century Swiss theologian Oscar Cullmann. Like others before him, Cullmann understood that the Jewish notion of the two ages formed an important background for understanding the message of Jesus. According to Judaism, history is divided into two periods: this age of sin and the age to come (the kingdom of God). For Jews the advent of the Messiah will effect the shift from the former to the latter age. In other words, Judaism viewed the two ages as consecutive.

According to Cullmann, Jesus Christ announced that the end of time, the kingdom of God, had arrived *in* history (see Mark 1:15 and parallels, especially Luke 4:43; 6:20; 7:28; 8:1, 10; 9:2, 11, 27, 60, 62; 10:9, 11; 11:20; 13:18, 20; 16:16; 17:20–21; 18:16–17, 24–25, 29). Yet other passages suggest that, although the age to come had *already* dawned, it was *not yet* complete. It awaited the second coming for its full realization (Luke 13:28–29; 14:15; 19:11; 21:31; 22:16, 18; 23:51; Acts 1:6), hence the term "inaugurated" eschatology. Such a view is pervasive in the New Testament beyond the Gospels (see, for example, Acts 2:17–21; 3:18, 24; 1 Cor. 15:24; 1 Tim. 4:1; 2 Tim. 3:1; Heb. 1:2; 1 John 2:18). So according to inaugurated eschatology, the two ages are simultaneous: the age to come exists in the midst of this present age. Therefore Christians live in between the two ages until the parousia (second coming of Christ).

The preceding data in the Synoptics regarding the already/not-yet aspects of the kingdom of God can be broken down as follows: Mark, perhaps the first Gospel to be written, records Jesus's programmatic statement in 1:15: "The time is fulfilled, and the kingdom of God is at hand" (KJV). Then the Gospel, along with Luke and Matthew, goes on to demonstrate that Jesus's miracles, teachings, death, and resurrection inaugurated the kingdom of God. Yet it is also clear from Matthew, Mark, and Luke that the final manifestation of the kingdom has not yet happened. We may draw on Luke as an example of the other two Synoptics. Thus the third Gospel indicates that the kingdom was present in Jesus (Luke 7:28; 8:10; 10:9–11; 11:20; 16:16; 17:20–21), but it also awaited the return of Christ for its completion (Luke 6:20–26; 11:2; 12:49–50, 51–53; 13:24–30; 21:25–28; 22:15–18, 30). The same dual aspect of the kingdom pertains to Luke's second volume, Acts. The kingdom was present in Jesus's ministry and, now, through his disciples (Acts 1:3; 8:12; 19:8; 20:25; 28:23–31); but it will not be completed until Christ comes again (Acts 1:6; 14:22).

A Summary of Millenarianism in Church History

It's time now for us to take a step back and get the big picture of eschatology and apocalypticism—in short, millenarianism—by seeing what church history has to say about the subject. A couple of healthy things result when we do that. First, we get a sense of security from examining the eschatology of the church because we discover that this is a topic that has been discussed and debated by Christians for more than two thousand years and will probably be discussed and debated for many more years to come. Thus we don't need to panic when we meet someone on the street holding a sign saying, "The end of the world is near!" It doesn't look like God's good earth is going anywhere too fast (though I could be wrong on that). So we can relax a little bit when thinking about the issues.

Second, studying the various millennial interpretations held by the church throughout its history also is healthy because it instills in us a sense of humility. We learn that our particular eschatological theory is not the only "kid on the block." Other views of the end times have been around a long time too. This realization will make us patient with others.

I will offer a brief overview of the church's view of end-time prophecy by summarizing four broad historical periods: the Church Fathers (premillennial), the Medieval Church (amillennial), the Reformation Church (postmillennial), the

Modern Church (eclectic).[5] We will see that in each period of the church the second coming of Christ and the millennium were viewed through the lens of the politics of the day and the sociological status of the church at the time. Then the bulk of this book will focus on the thinking of the various eschatological views in reference to how the New Testament/early church of the first century portrays the millennium, especially in Revelation 20.

The Church Fathers—Second to Fourth Centuries

Though there were exceptions to the rule (Dionysius in the third century and Eusebius in the fourth century), most of the Patristic ("fathers") writers were premillennial in orientation. Papias (60–130), a bishop in Asia Minor, had personal contact with the disciples of Jesus, especially John. He stated that the Lord used to teach concerning the end times that Christ would return visibly, resurrect the dead, and set up a literal one-thousand-year, blissful rule on earth. Like many in his day, Papias called the millennium the "kingdom of Christ," rather than the "kingdom of God." This was so because the kingdom of Christ was thought to be his temporary reign on earth (Revelation 20), which would give way to the kingdom of God of the eternal state in the new heaven and new earth (Revelation 21–22). According to Papias, this was what the apostle John meant in Revelation 20–22.

The Epistle of Barnabas (second century) maintained that the six days of creation are actually a period of six thousand years because a thousand years are like one day to God (2 Peter 3:8). Thus after six thousand years of world history, Christ will come a second time and establish the millennium—a thousand-year Sabbath rest on the earth. Hippolytus (170–236) took a similar tack concerning the millennium, also believing it will be a Sabbath rest.

Irenaeus (130–200), bishop of Lyons in Southern Gaul (modern-day France), was taught by Polycarp, the disciple of the apostle John. In his *Against Heresies*, book 5, chapter 32, Irenaeus made a strong case for premillennialism. There he interprets Revelation 20 as predicting Christ's future, one-thousand-year rule on earth that restores paradise lost, resurrects the righteous, and bases its operation in Jerusalem (Rev. 20:1–6). After Christ's millennial reign, the final judgment will take place (vv. 7–15). For Irenaeus this literal, even crass, interpretation of the millennium was in the face of the Gnostics—those professing Christians who denied the humanity of Jesus's incarnation! But according to Irenaeus, not only was the incarnation real, so will be the millennium.

Justin Martyr (100–165, called a martyr because he witnessed to Christ by his life's blood), the great second-century apologist for the gospel, told Trypho, a Jewish critic of Christianity, that he believed in the second coming of Christ, which will bring about, "A resurrection of the dead and a thousand years in Jerusalem, which will then be built, adorned and enlarged."[6]

Tertullian (160–220), a leading theologian from North Africa, stressed that at his second coming Christ will set up his millennial kingdom in Jerusalem.

Other well-known premillennialists during the Patristic period included Methodius (260–311), Victorinus (d. 304), Commodianus (250s), and Lactantius (250–325). Even the heretic Montanus in about 170 predicted that Christ would soon return to Pepuza, a small town in Asia Minor, to set up his one-thousand-year rule on earth. Montanus's ascetic lifestyle and theological error (he thought he was the embodiment of the Holy Spirit!) managed to get him ousted by the church, but, still, his voice is further testimony to the premillennial interpretation that dominated the early Church Fathers.

Concluding the summary of the millenarianism of the Patristic period, I want to make two observations. First, the Church Fathers interpreted Revelation 20 literally because they essentially inherited that hermeneutic from their Jewish kinsmen. Jews at the time of Jesus and into the early Christian centuries read their Old Testament rather straightforwardly. Even Jewish theologians longed for the Messiah to come and establish a literal, albeit temporary, kingdom in Jerusalem (see Isa. 40–66; cf. *1 Enoch* 93:3–17 [150 BC]; *4 Ezra* 7:26–44/12:31–34 [AD 70]; *Apocalypse of Baruch* 29:3–30:140 [AD 100]). Interestingly enough, when the church pretty much broke with its Jewish heritage in the fourth century, it stopped interpreting Revelation 20 literally. We will see why in the summary of the Medieval Church.

Second, since the early Church Fathers believed that the second coming of Christ would bring on a literal millennial rule, they knew, obviously, that it had not yet happened. Instead, they were in a fight for their lives with the Roman Empire, which tried to stamp out Christianity as a rival religion to the worship of Caesar. Christians who confessed that Jesus, not Caesar, is Lord could not be tolerated. So the political persecution of the day created the maligned status of the church, a situation that could hardly be confused with the millennium. Even more, the Patristics believed themselves to be in the throes of the tribulation that John predicted would fall on the church (Revelation 6–18). Apparently, as of that time, the concept of a secret rapture whereby Christ would whisk away the church to heaven before the end-time tribulation fell on the earth had not occurred to the early Church Fathers. That was an idea whose time had not yet come. To put it another way, the early Church Fathers focused on the not-yet side of eschatology.

The Medieval Church—Fifth to Fifteenth Centuries

The Medieval Church focused on the already and not-yet aspects of eschatology. That is, they believed the kingdom of God had already arrived at the first coming of Christ but that it was not yet complete; this awaited the second coming. The amillennial interpretation exchanged a future, literal one-thousand-year utopia on earth for a present, spiritual kingdom of God in the church. The *a* in amillennial means *no* literal millennium! Through three individuals this view held firm control in the church for more than twelve centuries. They were Origen, Emperor Constantine, and above all Augustine.[7]

Origen (185–254) cast doubt on chiliasm (*chilias* is the Greek word for one thousand or millennium). To begin with, he advocated a spiritual/figurative interpretation of Scripture—the allegorical method. This new hermeneutic was much different from the literal reading of the Bible that Judaism bequeathed to Christianity. The allegorical, Platonic interpretation, combined with Origen's low estimate of the material world, along with his view that history is cyclical not linear, prompted him to question the idea of a future kingdom of material prosperity and carnal happiness. Thus the seed was sown in Origen's teaching that would bloom into full-blown amillennialism later in the church.

But none of this would have been possible without the Roman emperor Constantine (275–337). His Edict of Toleration in 313 led to the legalizing of Christianity, indeed in making Christianity the main religion of the empire. Others have written of Constantine on this point:

> He gave the Lateran Palace to the bishop of Rome, legalized the giving of monetary gifts to churches, began the construction of church buildings, and supported clergy, single women, and widows from public funds. Thus, fewer Christians were inclined to regard Rome as a force of evil and the emperor as the Antichrist. Moreover, millennialists had predicted that Christ would return and end the persecution of the church, but this did not harmonize with the events that had transpired. The millennial hope had thrived while people were under the pressure of persecution, but now in the newly "Christianized" Roman world, official hostility was past and there was a lessened need for such endtime teaching. The time was ripe for a new eschatology to replace chiliasm.[8]

Augustine (354–430), like Origen and Tyconius before him (d. 390), put a spiritual spin on the millennium. In his *City*

26

of God, Augustine maintained that Revelation 20 is actually describing the present age into which the kingdom of God has entered through the church. The first resurrection is the conversion of the sinner and the second resurrection will be the return of Christ. The twelve tribes ruling the world is the present church, the new and true Israel. The binding of Satan began with the preaching of the gospel by the church. Thus Augustine did not speak of an Antichrist or a rule of evil. Rather, Christ reigns now through his church. One source encapsulates what we have been saying about Augustine's amillennialism:

> Augustine spiritualized the millennium—hence he denied that there would be a literal reign of Christ on earth at some point in the future. Instead, during the present age the "city of God" exists alongside the "city of man," that is, the world. There are two distinct societies of people: one will reign eternally with God and the other will suffer eternal punishment. The earthly city is that of Cain and the heavenly one is that of Abel. Now the city of God is the church, and its citizens are repentant and forgiven sinners. The citizens of the earthly city are destined to never-ending punishment with the devil. This godless city is the "beast coming out of the sea" (Rev. 13:1). When Christ came the first time, he placed Satan in chains. However, in spite of the devil's limited power, he is still able to seduce people. When he is set free at the end of the age, he will regain his full powers and launch a final persecution. The wicked nations, symbolized by Gog and Magog, will attack the city of God, but they will be defeated. The dead will be raised, all will be judged, and the unrighteous will be consigned to everlasting torment. The faithful will be given new bodies, both physical and spiritual, and they will enjoy endless happiness with God.[9]

Thus the kingdom of God rules in the church of Christ between his first and second comings, and the church—the city of God—would stand long after the Roman Empire fell.

27

The Reformation and Its Influence—Sixteenth to Nineteenth Centuries

Amillennialism ruled the church's interpretation of Revelation throughout the Medieval period, but during the Protestant Reformation and beyond, a new view of the millennium would begin—postmillennialism. This approach emerged as interpreters became fascinated with the literal details of eschatology. With the outrage of Martin Luther (1483–1546) against the papacy of his day came a certain return to the literal reading of the Bible. This affected Luther's interpretation of Revelation, which the reformer used to equate the Antichrist with the pope and his beastly reign over the church and the world. So Luther's new hermeneutic of the future juggled the amillennial view (the kingdom of God reigns now in the true, reformed church) and the premillennial view (there is a literal Antichrist—the pope—who attacks Christ's church). When the Protestant Reformation began to sweep over Europe and beyond, many believed it had brought on the millennium, especially in the form of Puritanism.

Postmillenarianism came to full expression in the writings of Daniel Whitby (1638–1725), rector of St. Edmund's Church, Salisbury, who published the two-volume *Paraphrase and Commentary on the New Testament* in 1703. He held that the earth's population would be converted to Christ, the Jews restored to the Holy Land, the pope and Turks vanquished, and then the world would enjoy a thousand-year golden age of universal peace, happiness, and righteousness. At the close of this period, Christ would personally come to earth, and the last judgment would take place. Whitby's more optimistic outlook continued to be influential as his work was reprinted into the mid-nineteenth century.[10]

One of the most brilliant American philosophers and theologians of all time, Jonathan Edwards (1703–58), best-known to students of American literature as the author of the sermon "Sinners in the Hands of an Angry God," also adopted postmillennialism. For three decades he kept a journal on the book of Revelation in which he analyzed its contents, took notes from commentators, and recorded the signs of the times that he believed were leading to the millennium. He also set forth his millennial ideas in *Some Thoughts Concerning the Present Revival of Religion in New England* (1742) and the sermons of 1739 posthumously published in 1744 as *A History of the Work of Redemption*. These writings, which grew out of the revivals of the Great Awakening of the 1740s, painted a postmillennial vision on the landscape of the New World.

Edwards stated that the preaching of the gospel would achieve a golden age on earth. Edwards identified the fifth bowl judgment of Revelation with the eventual destruction of the papacy—the Antichrist—by the message of the Protestant Reformation. Edwards predicted this would happen in either 1866 or 2016. He thought the Great Awakening in America that he was experiencing was the prelude to the millennial kingdom. At that time heresy, infidelity, and superstition would be destroyed, along with Islam. The Jews would be converted and the heathen won to Christ. It would be a time of peace, immense learning, and holiness. At the end of the millennium, there would be a final, temporary rebellion against God, but Christ would crush the revolt when he returned at the end of history.[11]

With hindsight one can see the reason postmillennialism arose when it did—the eighteenth and nineteenth centuries were brimming with optimism and confidence. The triumph of the Protestant Reformation, the sense of "manifest destiny" that accompanied America's great strides, the spiritual revivals that swept England and America, not to mention the hope of scientific progress that Darwinian evolution boasted, all produced an unbridled enthusiasm that gave birth to the postmillennial interpretation. Its motto was "Every day in every way, man is getting better and better." This was the "already" aspect of eschatology. Such optimism, however, did not reign in the twentieth century: World War I, the Liberal-Fundamentalist debate, the Great Depression, World War II, and the threat of nuclear annihilation ever since have dashed the hopes of any imminent utopia and, with it, postmillennialism.

The Modern Church—Twentieth and Twenty-first Centuries

The modern church has witnessed the reemergence of the major millennial interpretations from the past, along with some new ones: premillennial, amillennial, postmillennial, skeptical, and eclectic. In chapters 2–6, I will develop these interpretations, along with their varying philosophies of the twentieth and twenty-first centuries. These have left the modern interpreter in a millennial maze, with seemingly no escape from its confusion.

Conclusion

We have come a long way already in our study of end-time prophecy—from the Old Testament to the New Testament to the Patristic period to the Medieval Church to the Reformation era to today. And we have seen that there is a wrong way and a right way to interpret eschatology. Essentially, the wrong way to interpret biblical prophecy is to read anachronistically the current events of our day back into the Scripture. This approach runs the risk of obscuring what the sacred authors had to say for their day. The right way to understand end-time prophecy is to recognize the already/not-yet aspects of eschatology and the kingdom of God. The kingdom of God has already dawned with the first coming of Christ, but it is not yet complete. The latter aspect awaits the return of Christ. This dynamic will become the key to negotiating the confusion of millennial interpretations. To that topic we now turn.

2

Thy Kingdom Come

The Premillennial View of End-Time Prophecy

The Lord's Prayer hits the nail on the prophetic head when it comes to the premillennial view of the kingdom of God:

> Our Father in heaven,
> hallowed be your name,
> your kingdom come,
> your will be done
>   on earth as it is in heaven.
> Give us today our daily bread.
> Forgive us our debts,
>   as we also have forgiven our debtors.
> And lead us not into temptation,
> but deliver us from the evil one.
>
>   Matthew 6:9–13

For the premillennialist, the kingdom of God is almost totally futuristic, not that some in this school of thought don't subscribe to the already/not-yet aspects of the kingdom of God described earlier. To better grasp the premillennial understanding of end-time prophecy, let us compare and contrast the Jewish and Christian perspectives regarding the kingdom of God and the two ages.

According to Jewish thought at the time of the New Testament, history is divided into two ages: this evil age and the millennial age to come. This present age is characterized by sin and suffering, thanks to Adam and Eve's sin in the Garden of Eden. It is devoid of the Holy Spirit. But when the Messiah comes, he will establish the age to come, or the kingdom of God, on earth. That will be an unprecedented time of righteousness and wholeness. Thus, according to Jewish thinking, the two ages are consecutive: this age—the kingdom of men—will give way to the age to come—the kingdom of God. This abrupt change will happen when the Messiah arrives on earth. Thus:

Old Jewish View

The Present Age	The Coming Age (or the Kingdom of God)
The time of Satan	The time of God
Sin, sickness, and death	*Righteousness, wholeness, and eternal life*
No Spirit of God	*God's Holy Spirit*

But Jesus the Messiah dramatically "tweaked" the Jewish view of the two ages. His first coming launched the kingdom of God on earth within people's hearts during this present evil age, as his miracles, death, and resurrection showed. Thus forgiveness now belongs to those whose faith is in Christ, and God's kingdom is making significant inroads into the kingdom of Satan through the power of the Spirit. Yet the kingdom of God/age to come is not complete. The Christian and the church still must fight the good fight of faith until Christ comes again. In other words, the Christian lives between this age and the age to come. Thus:

The Christian View of the End

In-breaking of kingdom		Consummation
The present age	Between the times	The coming age
The time of "the flesh"		The time of the Spirit

As already mentioned, premillennial interpreters (some anyway) accept this construct as the key to understanding the kingdom of God, but they focus on the not-yet aspect. The kingdom of God did dawn, but more so in heaven than on earth. Only at the second coming will the kingdom of God be fully manifested on earth.

With the preceding in mind, we now examine the premillennial school of thought. We will begin by presenting its arguments for a future, literal reign of Christ on earth for a thousand years. Then we will further examine the premillennial interpretation by looking at its three varieties: pretribulationist, posttribulationist, and midtribulationist.

The Premillennial School of Thought

Often advocates of the idea of a future, literal millennial kingdom put forth four arguments in defense of their position. First, they interpret the Abrahamic Covenant literally and unconditionally (Gen. 12:1–3; 15:18–21; 17:7–8). That is, God's promise to Abraham that his seed would inherit the land of Israel has never been revoked (see also Isaiah 40–66; Jer. 29:1–14; Dan. 9:2). So the church has not permanently replaced Israel in the plan of God. This is so especially for the pretribulationist variety of premillennialism; see below. The day is coming when Israel will convert to Jesus as their Messiah. When Jesus returns from heaven to establish the millennium, Jerusalem will serve as his base of operations and Jewish Christians will play a leading role at that time (Rom. 11:25–27; Revelation 7; 14).

33

Second, the idea of a temporary millennial kingdom is attested to in at least three Jewish apocalyptic works basically contemporaneous with the New Testament: 1 Enoch 93:3–17 (ca. 150 BC); *4 Ezra* 7:26–44/12:31–34 (ca. AD 90); and *Apocalypse of Baruch* 29:3–30:1/40:1–4/72:2–74:3 (ca. AD 100). Each of these writings envisions the following scenario: *this age—temporary messianic kingdom—eternal age to come/kingdom of God.* In the above Jewish texts, the Messiah will come and form a transitional kingdom between this age and the age to come. Some ancient rabbis held to the same belief (Akiba, ca. AD 135; Eliezer b. Hurcanus, ca. AD 90; Jehoshua, ca. AD 90).

Third, Paul seems to allude to the temporary messianic kingdom in 1 Corinthians 15:20–28. Some scholars have synthesized Paul's view of the sequence of eschatological events in the following way:

1. the sudden and unexpected parousia (second coming, 1 Thess. 5:1–4)
2. the resurrection of deceased believers and the transformation of living believers, all of whom meet the Lord in the air (1 Thess. 4:16–17)
3. the messianic judgment presided over by Christ (2 Cor. 5:10) or God the Father (Rom. 14:10)
4. the dawn of the messianic kingdom (not described in detail by Paul but perhaps hinted at in 1 Cor. 15:24–28; Gal. 4:26)
5. during the messianic kingdom, the transformation of all nature from mortality to immortality (Rom. 8:19–22), and a struggle with angelic powers (Rom. 16:20) until death itself is conquered (1 Cor. 15:23–28)
6. the end of the messianic kingdom (Paul does not mention its duration)
7. a general resurrection at the end of the messianic kingdom (1 Cor. 15:24–28; cf. 6:3)
8. immediate judgment on all men and defeated angels

According to this proposal, Paul introduced two resurrections—one at the return of Christ and the other at the end of the messianic kingdom. This modification of Jewish eschatology was motivated by the life, death, and resurrection of Jesus the Messiah. The first resurrection will enable believers to participate in the messianic kingdom, all the while enjoying a resurrection mode of existence.

Fourth, the key New Testament passage that is thought by premillennialists to teach the temporary messianic kingdom is Revelation 20. According to this view, Christ will return at the end of the tribulation (Revelation 6–19) to defeat Satan, the Antichrist, and their minions and throw them into the bottomless pit for a thousand years. The absence of God's enemies will result in an unprecedented era of peace on the earth as Christ rules from Jerusalem (20:1–3). Along with Christ, Christians will rule in the millennial kingdom (vv. 4–6). After the completion of the thousand years, Satan will be released temporarily for the purpose of deceiving the nations into joining him for one last stand against God and his Christ—the battle of Gog and Magog. However, Christ will destroy Satan and sin forever, casting them into the lake of fire at the great white throne judgment (vv. 7–15). These events will be followed by the final state or the eternal kingdom of God.

Often non-premillennialists raise two objections to the proposal of a temporal millennial kingdom. First, they argue that only the martyrs of the end-time tribulation are referred to as reigning with Christ (v. 4), thus ruling out the entire church's reign with Christ at that time. Second, they view the resurrection mentioned in Revelation 20:4–6 as spiritual and not physical in nature. It is conversion that is being referred to here, not bodily resurrection. In response, premillennialists counter by observing that the resurrection of the martyrs does not occur until later, thus distinguishing them from the general populace of Christians, who also co-reign with Christ (v. 4). In addition, elsewhere in Revelation John promises that the faithful, not just the martyrs, will share Christ's future reign (2:26–28; 3:12, 21; 5:9–10; see also 1 Cor. 6:2–3).

The second response of those who defend Revelation 20 as teaching a millennial kingdom is that a spiritual resurrection can hardly compensate the martyrs mentioned in Revelation 20:4, because they are still physically dead even though spiritually alive in the presence of the Lord. Rather, what they need is a bodily resurrection. Furthermore, the Greek verb *ezesan* ("they lived") in Revelation 20:4 refers to a bodily resurrection, for a number of reasons: (a) the same verb in 20:5 means bodily resurrection; (b) the related root verb *zao* ("I live") frequently in Revelation refers to bodily resurrection (1:18; 2:8; 13:14; 20:5); (c) in the context of death *zao* always refers to physical resurrection in the New Testament (John 11:25; Acts 1:3; 9:41); and (d) John clearly equates "live" with resurrection in Revelation 20:5. In Revelation 20:5, "live" is the Greek word *anastasis*, which is used more than forty times in the New Testament with reference to physical resurrection.

These considerations are put forth in the premillennial reading of Revelation 20.

Intimately associated with premillennialism is its view that the history of the world should be interpreted pessimistically. Stanley J. Grenz summarized this interpretation:

> In contrast to the optimism of postmillennialism, premillennialism displays a basic pessimism concerning history and the role we play in its culmination. Despite all our attempts to convert or reform the world, prior to the end antichrist will emerge and gain control of human affairs, premillennialism reluctantly predicts. Only the catastrophic action of the returning Lord will bring about the reign of God and the glorious age of blessedness and peace. In keeping with this basic pessimism concerning world history, premillennial theologies emphasize the discontinuity, or even the contradiction between, the present order and the kingdom of God, and they elevate the divine future over the evil pres-

ent. The kingdom is the radically new thing God will do. However it may be conceived, the "golden age"—the divine future—comes as God's gracious gift and solely through God's action.[1]

Survey of Revelation 20

The eschatological drama of Revelation 20 unfolds in four acts: the temporary binding of Satan (vv. 1–3), the enthronement of the martyrs (vv. 4–6), the release of Satan and the end-time holy war (vv. 7–10), the eternal judgment at the great white throne (vv. 11–15).

The Temporary Binding of Satan (vv. 1–3)

In John's vision, an angel descended from heaven with a key to the Abyss (the bottomless pit below the surface of the earth reserved for Satan and his demons) and a chain. The use of chains to bind Satan and his hosts is an apocalyptic motif (*1 Enoch* 54:3–5; *2 Apoc. Bar.* 56:13; *Sib. Or.* 2.289; Jude 6; cf. 2 Peter 2:4) and may derive from earlier Greek traditions that record the binding of the Titans in Tartarus (Hesiod, *Theog.* 718; Hyginos, *Fabulae* 15c). Satan's aliases are used—"dragon," "serpent," "devil," "Satan" (compare Rev. 20:2 with 12:3–4, 7, 9, 13, 16–17; 13:2, 4). The binding of Satan and casting him into the Abyss is essentially an exorcism (see *1 Enoch* 10:4, 11–12; 13:1; 14:5; 18:16; 21:3–6; *Jub.* 5:6; 10:7–11; *2 Apoc. Bar.* 56:13; Jude 6; cf. 2 Peter 2:4). The Abyss—bottomless pit—seems to refer to a temporary subterranean place of incarceration for fallen angels at the present time (Jude 6; 2 Peter 2:4) and for Satan at the end of time (Rev. 20:1–3), analogous to the Greek idea of Tartarus. The temporary Abyss will itself be eventually thrown into the eternal lake of fire (vv. 7–15). While this scene could be a dramatization of Christ's defeat of Satan at the cross (see the amillennial view), the mention in verse 3 that Satan will not be able to deceive the nations for a thousand years is more likely understood by John as a literal event to occur in the near future, for obviously it had not happened by John's day. Christ will return (19:11–21) and cast Satan into the Abyss for one thousand years. This will provide unprecedented peace and harmony on earth for that period of time—the millennium. After that temporary period, Satan will be released (implied, by God) for the purpose of staging one last, brief stand for evil (20:3).

The Enthronement of the Martyrs (vv. 4–6)

There is much debate over the identification of the thrones and those who were seated on them that John sees, with three possibilities emerging. They may be heavenly thrones on which angels sit (cf. Dan. 7:9–10); martyrs who are singled out for special privilege by sitting on thrones and reigning with Christ while the rest of humanity (Christians included) await the general resurrection at the end of the millennium (cf. Dan. 7:22a); or all the saints who will reign with Christ during the millennium. The premillennialist believes the last option is the most nearly correct.

Revelation 20:5b–6 calls for two observations. The "first resurrection" suggests several resurrections. Thus the "first stage" of the first resurrection was that of Christ (1:18; cf. 1 Cor. 15:23–28), while the second stage will be that of Christians martyred at the hands of the Antichrist (Rev. 20:4), which probably will include all Christians as well. Though not called such, it is implied that there will be a "second resurrection"— the general resurrection of non-Christians to be sentenced to eternal judgment (vv. 12–13).

The second observation is that, while "the second death" is mentioned (v. 6), there is no reference to a "first death," but that too is implied here. "First death" would be a reference to physical death while "second death" refers to eternal, spiritual death. Most likely, John used "second death" as the description in verse 6 in contrast to the term "first resurrection" in verses 5 and 6.

The Release of Satan and the End-Time Holy War (vv. 7–10)

Verses 7–10 tell of the dramatic release of Satan and the end-time Holy War. The paragraph raises three questions. The first is, who are Gog and Magog (vv. 7–8a)? The terms *Gog* and *Magog* allude to Ezekiel 38–39 and the prophet's prophecy therein that a hostile nation from the north (38:4–6, 15–39:2) will attack peaceful Israel in the latter days (38:8–16), but that enemy nation will be destroyed by God (38:17–23; 39:1–6).

Interpreters have understood Revelation 20:7–10 in several ways: (1) Gog and Magog make up a *demonic* army. (2) Gog and Magog represent the rest of the dead who are resurrected and judged. (3) The destruction narrated in 19:17–21 does not include *all* the inhabitants of the earth, so the forces led by Gog and Magog are the *rest*. (4) The use of mythical, metaphoric language in 20:7–10 means that one need not necessarily follow the logic of the narrative. Probably view 3 is to be preferred. Beyond that, the careful interpreter will not say.

If view 3 above is correct, then it would help provide an answer to a second question raised by this text: where did the nations come from that Satan deceived (v. 8)? In the view above, Gog and Magog would be "leftovers" from the battle of Armageddon (Rev. 19:17–21). Perhaps, then, those nations will propagate people during the millennial kingdom. Also the huge number, "like the sand of the seashore," reminds one of the attack on Jerusalem by the nations in the end time and God's defeat of them (see Psalms 46; 48; 76; Ezekiel 38–39; cf. *4 Ezra* 13:5).

A third question is, what is the beloved city (v. 9)? Most likely the beloved city is Jerusalem. The "camping of God's people" would then be the messianic army gathered outside the city's walls ready to defend the holy city; or the camp could be the beloved city itself. When Satan and the nations surround the holy city, God will utterly destroy them. Modern readers of this passage might well think of that climactic battle in the Lord of the Rings:

> But Gandalf lifted up his arms and called once more in a clear voice: "Stand, Men of the West! Stand and wait! This is the hour of doom." And even as he spoke the earth rocked beneath their feet. Then rising swiftly up, far above the Towers of the Black Gate, high above the mountains, a vast souring darkness sprang into the sky, flickering with fire. The earth groaned and quaked. The Towers of the Teeth swayed, tottered, and fell down; the mighty rampart crumbled; the Black Gate was hurled in ruin; and from far away, now dim, now growing, now mounting to the clouds, there came a drumming rumble, a roar, a long echoing roll of ruinous noise. "The realm of Sauron is ended!" said Gandalf. "The Ring-bearer has fulfilled his Quest." And as the Captains gazed south to the Land of Moror, it seemed to them that, black against the pall of cloud, there rose a huge shape of shadow, impenetrable, lightning-crowned, filling all the sky. Enormous it reared above the world, and stretched out toward them a vast threatening hand, terrible but impotent: for even as it leaned over them, a great wind took it, and it was all blown away, and passed; and then a hush fell.[2]

It is interesting that John does not record any actual fighting on the part of the people of God in their stand against Gog and Magog. It is not clear if John thought they would fight or the battle would be the Lord's alone or some sort of combination. God sends his fire to destroy the nations. Then he will cast the devil, the beast (the Antichrist), and the false prophet into the eternal lake of fire (vv. 9b–10).

The Eternal Judgment at the Great White Throne (vv. 11–15)

After the put-down of the revolt of Satan and Gog and Magog, the throne of God appeared to John. God's throne is huge and white (compare v. 11 with 1 Kings 6:23–28; Isa. 6:1; *4 Ezra* 8:21). All the dead appeared before that throne (vv. 12–13). The phrase "books were opened" alludes to Daniel 7:10, probably with reference to two books: one for the deeds of the righteous and one for the deeds of the wicked (cf. Ps. 56:8; Isa. 65:6; Jer. 22:30; Mal. 3:16; *Jub.* 30:22; 36:10; *Asc.* 9:22; *Lev. Rab.* 26). The other book is the Book of Life (compare vv. 12–13 with Rev. 3:5; 13:8; 17:8; 20:15; 22:19). The deeds of the righteous proceed from their persevering in their faith in Jesus. The deeds of the unrighteous show that they had no faith in Christ (vv. 13–15). The wicked, along with death and Hades, will be cast into the eternal lake of fire (v. 15). This is the second death (see 2:11; 20:6; 21:8).

This, then, is the premillennial interpretation of Revelation 20. We now survey the three varieties of premillennialism.

Three Varieties of Premillennialism: Pretribulational, Posttribulational, and Midtribulational

People who hold to any one of the three varieties of premillennialism—pretribulational, posttribulational, midtribulational—believe Christ will return to earth for the purpose of establishing his literal one-thousand-year reign. There are conflicting interpretations, however, of whether the church will go through the end-time tribulation. Now we survey each of these views.

Pretribulation or Dispensationalism

The most popular interpretation of Revelation among American audiences during the twentieth century and into the present century has been dispensationalism, one of the varieties of premillennialism. The name of the movement is derived from the biblical term *dispensation*, which refers to the administration of God's earthly household (in the KJV: 1 Cor. 9:17; Eph. 1:10; 3:2; Col. 1:25). Dispensationalists divide salvation history into historical eras or epochs to distinguish the different administrations of God's involvement in the world. C. I. Scofield, after whom the enormously popular *Scofield Reference Bible* was named, defined a dispensation as "a period of time during which man is tested in respect of obedience to some specific revelation of the will of God."[3] During each dispensation, humankind fails to live in obedience to the divine test, consequently bringing that period under God's judgment and thus creating the need for a new dispensation. Read this way, the Bible can be divided into the following eight dispensations (though the number and names vary in this school of thought): innocence, conscience, civil government, promise, Mosaic law, church and age of grace, tribulation, millennium.

The hallmark of dispensationalism has been its commitment to a literal interpretation of prophetic Scripture. This has resulted in three well-known tenets cherished by adherents of the movement.

1. A distinction between the prophecies made about Israel in the Old Testament and the church in the New Testament must be maintained. In other words, the church has not replaced Israel in the plan of God. The promises he made to that nation about its future restoration will occur. The church is, therefore, a parenthesis in the outworking of that plan. (Recall my remarks on this point at the beginning of this chapter.) The dispensational distinction between Israel and the church was solidified in the minds of many as a result of two major events in the last century: the Holocaust (which rightly elicited deep compassion from many for the Jewish people) and the rebirth of the State of Israel in 1948. Dispensationalists appeal to Romans 11 in support of their view that God will convert the nation of Israel to Christ in the end time, for there Paul seems to say that Israel's present rejection of Jesus is only partial

(vv. 1–10). In the meantime, mercifully, Gentiles have the opportunity to accept Christ while the Jews don't (vv. 11–24), and God will convert the nation of Isael to Christ after the fullness of Gentiles have come in (11:25–27).

2. Dispensationalists are premillennialists; that is, they believe Christ will come again and establish a temporary, one-thousand-year reign on earth from Jerusalem.

3. Dispensationalists believe in the pretribulation rapture; that is, Christ's return will occur in two stages. The first one is for his church (the rapture), which will be spared the end-time tribulation; the second return is when Christ comes in power and glory to conquer his enemies.

Dispensationalism seems to have been first articulated by the Irish Anglican clergyman John Nelson Darby, an influential leader in the Plymouth Brethren movement in England during the nineteenth century. The movement was imported to the United States, receiving much recognition with the publication in 1909 of the *Scofield Reference Bible*. At least three developments unfolded within the movement during the last century. (1) The earliest development was propounded by Darby and Scofield, a period that identified and emphasized the dispensations themselves. (2) A second development emerged in the 1960s, thanks to Charles C. Ryrie's work *Dispensationalism Today*. With this second development, two noticeable changes transpired within dispensationalism. First, faith was highlighted as the means of salvation in any of the dispensations (contra the old *Scofield Bible*'s statement about works being the means of salvation in the Old Testament; see its footnote on John 1:17). The second change was that individual dispensations were no longer the focal point; rather, the emphasis now lay on the literal hermeneutic of dispensationalism. (3) In the 1980s there was a third development, the appearance of what is commonly called progressive dispensationalism. This variant

43

of dispensationalism adheres more closely to the already/not-yet eschatological tension. This approach allows it to root Revelation in the first century AD (especially the early church's struggle with the Roman imperial cult) while still holding to the futurity of the end-time tribulation, the parousia, and the millennium.

The classical dispensationalist's understanding of the time frame of Revelation and its structure go hand in hand. Because this school of thought interprets the prophecies of the book literally, their fulfillment, therefore, is perceived as still future (especially chaps. 4–22). Moreover, the magnitude of the prophecies (for example, one-third of the earth destroyed; the sun darkened) suggests that they have not yet occurred in history.

The key verse in this discussion is 1:19, particularly its three tenses, which are thought to provide an outline for Revelation: "what you have seen" (the past, John's vision of Jesus in chap. 1); "what is now" (the present, the letters to the seven churches in chaps. 2–3); "what will take place later" (chaps. 4–22). In addition, the classical dispensationalist believes that the lack of mention of the church from Revelation 4 on indicates that it has been raptured to heaven by Christ before the advent of the tribulation (chaps. 6–18).

Pretribulation Rapture

Christ comes for his church and takes them to heaven

Christ comes with his church to begin millennial reign

Church Age | Great Tribulation | Millennium | Eternal State

Christ comes for his church and takes them to heaven

Christ comes with his church to begin millennial reign

Resurrection of unbelievers for judgment

Dispensations in the Dispensational Tradition

J. N. Darby (1808–82)	J. H. Brookes (1830–97)	E. W. Bullinger (1837–1913)	C. I. Scofield (1843–1921)	I. M. Haldeman (1845–1933)	Wm. Graham Scroggie (1877–1958)
Paradisaical State	Innocence	Innocence	Innocence	Edenic	Adamic
Conscience	Conscience	Patriarchal	Conscience	Antediluvian	Antediluvian
Noah	Patriarchs		Human Government	Patriarchal	Noahian
Abraham			Promise		Patriarchal
Israel 1. Law 2. Priest 3. Kings Gentiles	Law	Law	Mosaic		Sinaitic 1. Mosaic 2. Gideonic 3. Davidic
	The Lord	Grace	Grace	Messianic	Christian
Spirit/ Christian Church	Grace			Holy Ghost	
		Judicial			
Millennium	Millennial Age	Millennial	Kingdom	Restitution	Millennial
		Glory		Eternal State	Final

Various identifications of the dispensations.[4]

Posttribulation or Historic Premillennialism

The historic premillennial interpretation agrees with its sibling viewpoint—dispensationalism—that Christ will return to establish a thousand-year reign on earth at his parousia. But sibling rivalry ensues between the two approaches on the issue of the relationship of the church and the end-time tribulation (Revelation 6–18). According to historic premillennialism,[5] the church will undergo the messianic woes—the end-time tribulation. This is so because the church has replaced Old Testament Israel as the people of God (see Rom. 2:26–28; 11;

45

Gal. 6:16; Eph. 2:11–22; 1 Peter 2:9–10; Rev. 1:5–6; 7:1–8). Like amillennialism, the historic premillennial view is based on the already/not-yet eschatological hermeneutic: the kingdom of God dawned with the first coming of Christ, but it will not be completed until the second coming of Christ. And in the between period the church encounters the messianic woes, which will intensify and culminate in the return of Christ.

So historic premillennialism does not distinguish between the rapture of the church in secret and the second coming of Christ in visible glory to earth. Rather, the two are perceived to be the same event, and this will occur *after* the seven-year end-time tribulation.

The pretribulational view appeals to two major arguments in its claim that the church will be raptured from the earth before the advent of the messianic woes/end-time tribulation:

1. First Thessalonians 4:13–18 distinguishes the rapture of the church from the parousia, the second coming of Christ in glory.
2. The church is not destined to undergo the wrath of God, which would happen if it has to go through the tribulation. God's wrath is reserved for unbelievers and will be poured out on the earth precisely in the form of the end-time tribulation (compare 1 Thess. 1:10; 5:9 with Rev. 6:16–17).

But the posttribulationist begs to differ with these two claims. Regarding the first, it is clear that 1 Thessalonians 4:13–18 (the rapture) matches descriptions of the second coming found in 1 Thessalonians 5; 2 Thessalonians 2; and the Olivet Discourse (see p. 63). Thus a comparison would look like the following.[6]

Olivet Discourse in Matthew	Event	Paul
24:5	warning about deception	2 Thess. 2:2

Olivet Discourse in Matthew	Event	Paul
24:5, 11, 14	lawlessness, delusion of the nonelect, signs, and wonders	2 Thess. 2:6–11
24:12	apostasy	2 Thess. 2:3
24:15	Antichrist in the temple	2 Thess. 2:4
24:21–22	tribulation preceding the end	2 Thess. 1:6–10
24:30–31	parousia of Christ, on clouds, at the time of a trumpet blast, with angelic accompaniment	1 Thess. 4:14–16
24:30–31	coming in power	2 Thess. 2:8
24:31	gathering of believers	1 Thess. 4:16; 2 Thess. 2:1
24:36, 42, 44, 50; 25:13	unexpected	1 Thess. 5:1–4
24:42–25:13	exhortation to watch!	1 Thess. 5:6–8

So the unavoidable conclusion here is that, if 1 Thessalonians 5; 2 Thessalonians 2; and the Olivet Discourse describe the parousia (which all interpreters believe they do), and if 1 Thessalonians 4:13–18 (the rapture) matches the previous texts on the second coming, then the "two" events are the same.

How then do we explain the relationship between the rapture and the second coming? Posttribulationists reply: the background to all of this is the Roman general's triumphant procession. This was a parade that Roman citizens held in honor of a Roman general's defeat of a significant enemy of the Roman Empire. When the general appeared (parousia means coming) on the horizon outside Rome, an entourage went out from the city to meet him and his army to escort them back into the city for the parade (see 1 Thess. 4:13–18). With the Roman general's triumphant procession as the backdrop to Christ's victorious descent to earth after defeating the Antichrist, the following scenario will play out according to the historic premillennial interpretation: the trumpet will sound

47

for the second coming of Christ at the end of the tribulation period. The church, Christ's entourage on earth during those messianic woes, will be caught up momentarily to meet Christ in the air for the purpose of escorting him to the earth in pomp and circumstance (1 Thess. 4:13–18—the rapture). Then he will descend to earth to celebrate his victory and establish his one-thousand-year reign (1 Thessalonians 5; 2 Thessalonians 2; Olivet Discourse; Revelation 19—the second coming).

Regarding the second claim, the posttribulationist agrees that the church will not undergo the wrath of God—but not because it is raptured to heaven before the tribulation falls on earth. Rather, God will protect the church from his wrath that falls on unbelievers during the messianic woes, just as he protected ancient Israel from the plagues he poured out on Egypt (see Revelation 8–9; 14–18; cf. Rev. 3:10).

The following chart, then, illustrates the posttribulational or historic premillennial perspective:

Midtribulation or Prewrath View

The third variety of premillennialism is a compromise between the pretribulational and posttribulational views, namely, the midtribulational interpretation. There are two expressions of this view: the traditional midtribulational view and the prewrath view.

Posttribulation Rapture

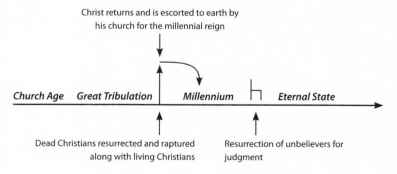

Christ returns and is escorted to earth by his church for the millennial reign

Church Age | Great Tribulation | Millennium | Eternal State

Dead Christians resurrected and raptured along with living Christians

Resurrection of unbelievers for judgment

THE MIDTRIBULATION RAPTURE VIEW

The midtribulation rapture view insists that the church will go through the first half of the end-time tribulation but will be removed prior to experiencing God's wrath poured out on earth during the second half of the end-time tribulation, called the Great Tribulation. Like posttribulationism, this view makes a distinction between tribulation and wrath. During the first three and one-half years of Daniel's seventieth week, the church will be present and experience the end-time tribulation. In this view the "elect" of Jesus's Olivet Discourse are the church rather than the Jews, as argued by pretribulationists. According to Matthew 24:21–22, the end-time tribulation will include the elect: "For then there will be great distress, unequaled from the beginning of the world until now—and never to be equaled again. If those days had not been cut short, no one would survive, but for the sake of the elect those days will be shortened" (v. 22). In Matthew 24:29 Jesus adds, "Immediately after the distress of those days the sun will be darkened, and the moon will not give its light; the stars will fall from the sky, and the heavenly bodies will be shaken." After the "distress" of the tribulation, God will pour out his wrath, as indicated by the severe judgments on the cosmos. Since the church will not experience God's wrath (Rom. 5:9; 1 Thess. 1:9–10; 5:9), the rapture of the church will occur at this midpoint of the seven-year, end-time tribulation (that is, just before God begins to pour out his wrath). In Revelation the rapture corresponds to the sounding of the seventh trumpet:

> The seventh angel sounded his trumpet. . . . We give thanks to you, Lord God Almighty, the One who is and who was, because you have taken your great power and have begun to reign. The nations were angry; and *your wrath has come*. The time has come for judging the dead, and for rewarding your servants the prophets and your saints and those who reverence your name, both small and great—and for destroying those who destroy the earth.
>
> Revelation 11:15, 17–18 (italics added)

49

The resurrection and catching up of the two witnesses in Revelation 11:11–12 represent the rapture of the church. Also midtribulationists see the woman's flight into the wilderness for "a time, times and half a time" in Revelation 12:14 as evidence for their view.

This halfway point of the tribulation is alluded to in Daniel 7:24–25, which says that "another king" different from the ten kings will "speak against the Most High and oppress his saints," and they "will be handed over to him for a time, times and half a time." Daniel also reveals that in the middle of the seven-year period (the middle of the seventieth week of years, or the Great Tribulation), the "abomination of desolation" will be set up in the temple (9:27). This is also what Paul has in mind when he speaks of the "man of lawlessness" setting himself up in God's temple (2 Thess. 2:3–9). Just before this time of wrath begins, God will rapture his church. Therefore, the rapture will occur three and one-half years into the end-time tribulation. The midtribulation view agrees with the pretribulation view that there will be two comings of Christ. Midtribulationists locate these two comings at the midpoint of the end-time tribulation (Christ's rapture of the church) and at the end of the outpouring of God's wrath (Christ's return to earth with the church).

The midtribulation rapture view attempts to take advantage of both the pretribulation and posttribulation views. With pretribulationism it argues for two second comings of Christ and for the rapture as a physical removal from God's wrath. With posttribulationism it prefers the more natural reading of "elect"—the church, not Israel—along with the admission that the church always has and always will endure tribulation, including end-time tribulation.

The weakness of the midtribulation view is the questionable restriction of God's wrath to the last half of the end-time tribulation, as well as the absence of direct biblical evidence for the rapture occurring in the middle of this period.[7]

Midtribulation Rapture

THE PREWRATH RAPTURE VIEW

The prewrath rapture view attempts to synthesize pre-, mid-, and posttribulational rapture views by refining the actual timing of the rapture in hopes of arriving at a harmonizing position. The prewrath view insists that the truth about the rapture will be some combination of the three established views. From pretribulationism the prewrath view accepts the truth that all believers will be exempt from the wrath of God. They do not, however, follow the pretribulation view in claiming that all seven years of the end-time tribulation include the outpouring of God's wrath.

With midtribulationism, the prewrath view maintains the distinction between the wrath of God poured out on the powers of evil and the wrath of Satan poured out on God's people. On the other hand, prewrath proponents cite Revelation 12:7–17 as evidence that Satan's wrath arrives during the second half of the seven-year tribulation (that is, the second half of Daniel's seventieth week, which equals forty-two months). This means that the wrath of God and the wrath of Satan overlap to some degree during this period.

Like posttribulationism, the prewrath view does not equate the "day of the Lord" and the end-time tribulation, but rather sees the day of the Lord coming at the end of the tribulation. The wrath of God will be restricted to the very last part of Daniel's seventieth week, that is, to the day of the Lord. Thus believers will be present during the Great Tribulation (the second half of the end-time tribulation), but they will not experience God's wrath because he will rapture the church at that point. The prewrath view does not accept the posttribulational position that believers will be present when God's wrath is poured out. Instead, they will be protected from his wrath.

The prewrath rapture view attempts to combine three elements from the established views along with a fourth element of its own:

1. The church is exempt from God's wrath.
2. There is a distinction between God's wrath and Satan's wrath.
3. There is a distinction between the Great Tribulation (the second half of the end-time tribulation) and the day of the Lord.
4. The wrath of Satan will be cut short by removing the object of his wrath through the rapture of the church and protection of a remnant of Israel to inhabit the millennial kingdom. This gap between the rapture of the church at the inception of the day of the Lord and Christ's coming in visible glory is the time when God's wrath is poured out through the trumpet and bowl judgments of Revelation.

Prewrath Rapture

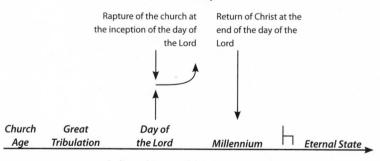

Rapture of the church at the inception of the day of the Lord

Return of Christ at the end of the day of the Lord

Church Age | Great Tribulation | Day of the Lord | Millennium | Eternal State

God's wrath is poured out on the day of the Lord

The strength of the prewrath rapture view lies in its attempt to build on the established views. It is most dependent on posttribulationism but stops short of having believers on earth when God's wrath is poured out, in spite of the fact that they would be spiritually protected. Whether this most recent of the rapture views can sustain exegetically its nuanced position without shifting into posttribulationism remains to be seen.[8]

Conclusion

The premillennial Lord's Prayer might go something like this:

Thy temporary, one-thousand-year kingdom come to earth (but this will happen only at the second coming of Christ)

So that Thy kingdom will accomplish on earth what it already has in heaven.

Lead us not into the temptation of the end-time tribulation, but deliver us from it by:

Not letting the church go through it at all (according to the "pretribbers").

Not letting the church go all the way through it (according to the "midtribbers"/"prewrathers").

Preserving the church during all of it (according to the "posttribbers").

The premillennial view, especially the pretribulation variety, is most popular among the American masses, thanks to the *Scofield Bible*, Hal Lindsey's *Late Great Planet Earth*, and the Left Behind series. But there are other ways to understand the end of the world as we know it. The next chapter will examine the most popular view among biblical scholars—the postmillennial school of thought.

3

Thy Kingdom Came

The Postmillennial View of End-Time Prophecy

The parousia of Christ! The second coming of Jesus! The return of the Lord! These are powerful, synonymous labels for end-time prophecy. Or are they? Not so, according to the postmillennial school of interpretation. Rather, the previous terms are symbolic descriptions of the coming of Christ to judge Jerusalem back in AD 70 by the hands of the Romans! How's that for a topsy-turvy reading of biblical prophecy? But there is more. According to many postmillennialists, the kingdom of God appeared with the first coming of Christ, whose death and resurrection signaled the end of the Jewish old covenant. And its replacement was the gospel of Jesus Christ, with a message that transformed the structures of society for righteousness' sake beginning in AD 33. In other words, the church of Christ brought on the millennium—which culminated in the coming again of Christ, the triumph of the kingdom of God through the preaching of the gospel in AD 70 to destroy Jerusalem, hence the title—postmillennium: Christ returned "post"—after—the millennium. Obviously this perspective emphasizes the already aspect of the kingdom of God.

Postmillennialism is tied into the preterist reading of Revelation. Preterism—Latin for "gone by" or "past"—interprets the book of Revelation, not as prophecy about the future end of the world but, rather, as prophecy about the return of Christ to judge Jerusalem, which occurred in AD 70. So the prophecies of Revelation were fulfilled in the first century, in connection with the Roman overthrow of Jerusalem. More on this particular point under Biblical Postmillennialism below.

Here we highlight the postmillennial view by way of a chart:

Postmillennialism

Christ comes after the millennium

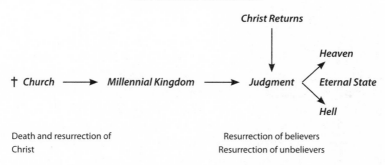

Here is how one notable postmillennialist unpacks the previous chart:

> Postmillennialism expects the proclaiming of the Spirit-blessed gospel of Jesus Christ to win the vast majority of human beings to salvation in the present age. Increasing gospel success will gradually produce a time in history prior to Christ's return in which faith, righteousness, peace, and prosperity will prevail in the affairs of people and of nations. After an extensive era of such conditions the Lord will return visibly,

bodily, and in great glory, ending history with the general resurrection and the great judgment of all humankind.[1]

Actually the postmillennial/preterist view is not unified; there is a liberal postmillennialism and a biblical postmillennialism. I will summarize these two views in the sections that follow. Interestingly enough, both of these viewpoints are based on a political mind-set. The former is championed by Barack Obama while the latter appealed to Ronald Reagan.

Liberal Postmillennialism

Liberal postmillennialism had its heyday in the nineteenth century in association with the "social gospel," whose mission was the liberation of humanity from societal evil (poverty, racism, disease, war, and injustice). The presupposition of this school of thought was that humanity is basically good and that ultimately society will get better and better, resulting in a golden age on earth. Laudable as this attempt was, however, the social gospel suffered from two flaws: it abandoned the preaching of the gospel, and it naively based its positive view of history on the Darwinian evolutionary process. Time dealt a mortal blow to liberal postmillennialism—the catastrophic events of the twentieth century (two world wars, the Great Depression, the threat of nuclear destruction by the world's superpowers or by terrorists or both) rendered it an untenable position.[2]

In this section we break down nineteenth-century liberal postmillennialism into its two parts: the social gospel and evolutionary theory. Interestingly enough, the twenty-first century has witnessed the revival of such a movement in the message of Barack Obama. In the next section we will focus on the biblical counterpart to liberal postmillennialism.

The Social Gospel

The social gospel of nineteenth-century America saw two problems with the gospel of Jesus Christ as preached by conservatives at that time: it was not social enough and it was too individualistic. Walter Rauschenbusch (1868–1918) sought to correct these two weaknesses with his message of the social gospel. Rauschenbusch once pastored in New York's notorious Hell's Kitchen. There he witnessed firsthand the poverty, violence, and despair unbridled capitalism could unleash on a people. Not unlike Karl Marx in that regard, Rauschenbusch believed that a capitalist-run government, with its self-interest and myopic agenda, is an obstacle to the progress of a nation rather than a means to its betterment. And as far as Rauschenbusch was concerned, the church of his day had sold its soul to corrupt government. No longer a prophetic voice for God and his people, the church had become the mouthpiece for institutional religion.

What was needed was the preaching of the kingdom of God, as Jesus preached it, so said Rauschenbusch. For him, this meant two things, two correctives to the traditional gospel as preached by conservatives. First, the kingdom of God is a goal-oriented concept. It looks forward to the transformation of the whole social order, not backward to the tradition and doctrine or dogma of the church. Thus the kingdom should not be reduced to the church. It is broader and better. So often the church helped to entrench evil institutions rather than reform or even replace them. The social gospel does the latter of these two possibilities: it seeks to reform or replace rather than entrench.

Second, "the kingdom is a fellowship of righteousness."[3] Therein lies the heart of the social gospel. It is ethical in nature—feeding the poor, caring for the sick, educating the illiterate, equalizing job opportunities, and so on. So salvation is not from sin, as conservatives preached, but from inequality and injustice. And we experience such salvation by loving our fellow humans as Jesus did. Moreover, the social gospel is corporate in nature—it is a "fellowship." Rauschenbusch, by now a professor of church history at Rochester Seminary, had come to believe that the problems of the poor and disadvantaged were not their own doing. That is, the problems were not individual in nature as conservatives had been preaching for years. Rather, the problems of the dispossessed were due to corrupt corporate structures. Thus the institutions themselves—capitalism, for example—had to be changed for the purpose of truly representing the good of the individual, not the reverse. Rauschenbusch put it this way: "The social gospel tries to see the progress of the kingdom of God in the flow of history . . . in the clash of economic forces and social classes, in the rise and fall of despotisms and forms of enslavement."[4]

Rauschenbusch could put it more bluntly: "The fundamental terms and ideas [associated with salvation as atonement from sin]—'satisfaction,' 'substitution,' 'imputation,' 'merit'—are post-biblical ideas, and are alien from the spirit of the gospel. . . . The problem of the social gospel is how the divine life of Christ can get control of human society."[5]

All of this sounds suspiciously similar to the successful presidential campaign platform of Barack Obama, who was nurtured in the "social gospel" (Obama's own words) message of Reverend Jeremiah Wright and Trinity United Church of Christ in South Chicago.

Evolutionary Theory

Armed with evolutionary theory, the social gospel packed a potent message. Charles Darwin's (1809–1882) theory of evolution provided the scientific backing for the social gospel's confidence in a brighter tomorrow. For Darwin, human development, morality, even religion are products of evolution. And although natural selection and the survival of the fittest might produce some "bumps" along the way, the road to utopia for planet Earth is sure and even imminent. The social gospel mantra that mankind was getting better every day in every way had "science" on its side.

There is much that was laudable about the social gospel. Its commitment to bettering the quality of human life; its confident trust that the kingdom of God will prevail over all evil contenders; its message of the need for the transformation of social structures for righteousness' sake; and its recognition that unchecked individualism is the death knell to the selfless message of Christianity are all praiseworthy concepts. But ultimately the social gospel as proclaimed by nineteenth-century liberal theologians failed miserably. By the end of the twentieth century, it had become only a whisper of a dream from bygone days—for three reasons.

First, the socialist, if not Marxist, tendency of the social gospel movement sabotaged its message. Rather than proliferating the gospel of the love of Jesus, Marxist regimes murdered millions and millions of dissidents, sacrificing them on the altar of a classless society. Little wonder, then, that Marxism itself stumbled and fell in the last quarter of the twentieth century.

Second, the evolutionary theory of progress that bolstered the social gospel also came increasingly under fire by scientists and nonscientists alike in the last century. The violence of natural selection, the degrading of human origins, the ravages of world wars, the Great Depression, the Holocaust, the threat of nuclear annihilation, not to mention the attempt to dethrone God, all cast grave doubt on a millennial utopia for planet Earth anytime soon.

Third, at the end of the day, the social gospel movement threw out the baby with the bathwater. That is, it discarded the traditional gospel and replaced it with a social gospel. But the message of twentieth-century evangelicalism was that we don't have to choose between the traditional gospel—that Jesus died for our sins and arose for our justification—and social justice. The two go hand in hand. Rooting their message in the Old Testament prophets and the work and words of Christ, evangelicals since the 1950s have rightly declared that the salvation from sin of one person at a time is the key to transforming society as a whole. So their message was and is that the true gospel is social in its ramifications, which, by the way, is something the Black Church in America has been saying for years.

Biblical Postmillennialism

Alongside liberal postmillennialism was its evangelical counterpart. Those theologians of the eighteenth and nineteenth centuries following this approach maintained their commitment to the gospel and to its transforming power. Stanley J. Grenz writes of them:

> Their outlook differed fundamentally from both secular and liberal Christian utopianism. They were optimistic concerning the future to be sure. But their optimism was born out of a belief in the triumph of the gospel in the world and of the work of the Holy Spirit in bringing in the kingdom, not out of any misconception concerning the innate goodness of humankind or of the ability of the church to convert the world by its own power.[6]

Today biblical postmillennialism has rebounded from the catastrophes of history and is currently experiencing a resurgence of influence, especially Christian Reconstructionism. Its conviction is admirable—as the church preaches the gospel and performs its role as the salt of the earth, the kingdom of God will advance until the whole world will one day gladly bow to the authority of Christ. The means for accomplishing this goal will be the law of God, which impacts the church and, in turn, the world.

Biblical postmillennialism has its origin in the likes of Daniel Whitby and Jonathan Edwards, as we saw earlier. It also boasts followers in such notable missionaries as William Carey (1761–1834), "Father of Modern Missions"; the old Princetonian theologians Charles Hodge (1797–1878) and B. B. Warfield (1851–1921); and Gresham Machen (1881–1937). But as we also noted earlier, with two world wars, the

Great Depression, the Holocaust, and the worldwide nuclear threat, postmillennialism fell into disfavor in the twentieth century. However, during the presidency of Ronald Reagan (1980–88), which brought renewed hope to many Americans, biblical postmillennialism made a comeback in the form of Christian Reconstructionism or theonomic ethics (*theonomy*, meaning "God's law"). Ken Gentry writes of this:

> The theonomic postmillennialist sees the *gradual* return to biblical norms of civil justice as a *consequence* of widespread gospel success through preaching, evangelism, missions, and Christian education. The judicial-political outlook of Reconstructionism includes the application of those justice-defining directives contained in the Old Testament legislation, when properly interpreted, adapted to new covenant conditions, and relevantly applied.[7]

Such an idea reminds one of the Puritans. Indeed, the Puritans are the heroes of Christian Reconstructionism. Thus enamored with the Puritan ethic and committed to the preaching of the traditional gospel, biblical postmillennialists demonstrated a positive view of where things are going prophetically: the world will get better and better because of the triumph of the gospel. In that sense, postmillennialism aligns itself with the role of the Old Testament prophet, whose message proclaimed the intervention of God in history, rather than with the apocalypticist's doom and gloom forecasts of the future.

Although some biblical postmillennialists believe that the parousia is still in the future, many hold to the preterist view that Christ's parousia already occurred—at the fall of Jerusalem to the Romans in AD 70. Therefore this group of interpreters reverses the commonly accepted position on the key passages in the debate—the Olivet Discourse, Revelation 1–19, and especially Revelation 20—by arguing that these passages refer to the past coming of Christ to judge Jerusalem, not some future coming of Christ to establish his kingdom in Jerusalem. We turn now to the preterist's summary of these biblical passages. After that, I will evaluate the biblical postmillennial position.

The Olivet Discourse

The Olivet Discourse is the sermon delivered by Jesus on the Mount of Olives forecasting the future of Israel and the world (Matthew 24; Mark 13; Luke 21). There are three general lines of interpretation of this sermon by Jesus regarding the coming signs of the times of his return. One is that Jesus is referring exclusively to his second coming at the end of history, in particular to the seven-year tribulation period. With this reading, taking Matthew as an example, verses 3–14 refer to the first three and a half years of the future tribulation period to be poured out on the earth while verses 15–31 refer to the second half of the tribulation period, often called the Great Tribulation. And immediately after the Great Tribulation comes the return of Christ and the millennium.

The second major interpretation of the Olivet Discourse is the already/not-yet dynamic. Thus Matthew 24:3–14 refers to the fall of Jerusalem in AD 70 (the already aspect) and is the backdrop to verses 15–31, the future second coming of Christ at the end of history to end the tribulation and establish his literal kingdom (the not-yet aspect). Recall the discussion of the already/not-yet approach in chapter 1.

The third view—postmillenialism/preterism—argues that the Olivet Discourse refers exclusively to the fall of Jerusalem to the Romans in AD 70. Thus the "generation" that will not pass away (v. 34) before all these things will be fulfilled was the generation that extended from Jesus's time (AD 30) to the fall of Jerusalem (AD 70) or forty years after the utterance of the Olivet Discourse. The signs of the times detailed in the Olivet Discourse, therefore, found their fulfillment in the horrors that fell on Jerusalem during the Roman siege of that city in AD 70 (see, for example, vv. 4–12).

Thus the false messiahs (see vv. 5, 23–24) were those Jewish pseudo-prophets who announced that God was about to deliver Jerusalem from the Romans and set up his kingdom in the "holy" city, predictions that proved to be false. The wars and rumors of wars refer to the Jewish revolt against Rome (AD 68–72), along with the civil wars that befell the Roman Empire between the death of Emperor Nero (AD 68) and the enthronement of Vespasian as emperor (AD 70—the same person who started the Roman campaign against Israel and then left it to his son Titus to finish the job). The famines were those that devastated Jerusalem during the Roman siege. The earthquakes refer to the apparently unprecedented seismic activity in the Roman Empire from AD 30 to 70, Judea included. The cosmic disturbances in the heavens (v. 29) were comets that occurred for all to see at that time, including a comet that hovered over Jerusalem like a sword during the Roman siege of the city. The tribulation was the persecution of the church by Jews and Romans (vv. 9–10). The lawlessness and apostasy of the period are descriptions of those professing Christians who left the faith rather than face persecution (v. 10). The coming of the Son of Man (vv. 30–31) was Jesus's judgment of Jerusalem and the destruction of its temple through the instrument of the Roman army.

Thus the postmillennialist argues that the signs of the times delineated in the Olivet Discourse found their fulfillment in and around AD 70.[8]

Revelation 1–19

The postmillennial interpretation of Revelation 1–19 restricts the fulfillment of the prophecies therein to the first century, which is in keeping with the name of this school of thought—preterist. The preterist viewpoint wants to take seriously the historical setting of Revelation by relating it to its author and audience. That is, the apostle John addressed his book to real churches that faced dire problems in the first century AD. It is thought that two quandaries in particular provided the impetus for the recording of the book. Kenneth L. Gentry Jr. writes of these:

> Revelation has two fundamental purposes relative to its original hearers. In the first place, it was designed to steel the first century Church against the gathering storm of persecution, which was reaching an unnerving crescendo of theretofore unknown proportions and intensity. A new and major feature of that persecution was the entrance of imperial Rome onto the scene. The first historical persecution of the Church by imperial Rome was by Nero Caesar from AD 64 to AD 68. In the second place, it was to brace the Church for a major and fundamental reorientation in the course of redemptive history, a reorientation necessitating the destruction of Jerusalem (the center not only of Old Covenant Israel, but of Apostolic Christianity [cf. Acts 1:8; 2:1ff.; 15:2] and the Temple [compare Matt. 24:1–34 with Revelation 11]).[9]

Thus the sustained attempt to root the fulfillment of the divine prophecies of Revelation in the first century AD constitutes the preterist's distinctive approach.

Preterists locate the timing of the fulfillment of the prophecies of Revelation in the first century AD, specifically just before the fall of Jerusalem in AD 70. Despite the opinion of many that Revelation was written in the 90s during the reign of Emperor Domitian (81–96), much of evangelical preterism holds the date of the book to be Neronian (54–68). Three basic arguments are put forth to defend this period:

1. There are allusions throughout Revelation to Nero as the current emperor (for example, 6:2; 13:1–18; 17:1–13).
2. The condition of the churches in Asia Minor to which John writes his letters (chaps. 2–3) best correlates with pre–AD 70 Jewish Christianity, a time that witnessed

the rupture between Christianity and Judaism. In effect, Revelation attests to the twofold persecution of Jewish Christianity—by the Jews and by the Romans. The former persecuted Jewish believers because of their faith in Jesus as the Messiah, so that they were consequently expelled from the synagogues, thus exposing them to Caesar worship. Jews were exempt from worshiping Caesar and so were Jewish Christians as long as they were associated with the synagogues. But when non-Christian Jews kicked out Christian Jews from the synagogues, the latter were no longer considered Jews by the Romans. Subsequently the Romans tried to force Jewish Christians to revere Caesar. Retaliating for this first-century Jewish persecution of Christians, John predicts that Christ will come in power to destroy Jerusalem, using the Roman Empire to do so (see, for example, 1:7–8; 2–3; 11; 17–18; 22:20)—a warning that came true with Jerusalem's fall in AD 70.

3. According to Revelation 11, the temple seems still to be standing (that is, at the time of the writing of the book).

With the preceding as background, here is a summary of the postmillennial/preterist reading of Revelation 1–19.

Revelation 1:1–3 predicts that the events of Revelation will happen soon, very soon, and they did—in AD 70, no more than two or three years after John recorded his heavenly visions. Revelation 1:7 predicts that these prophetic events coincided with the coming of Christ to judge Jerusalem. Revelation 2–3 records the trials and temptations of Jewish Christians in Asia Minor during the 60s AD, when non-Christian Jews betrayed their kinsmen (Jewish Christians) to the Roman authorities, who in turn persecuted Jewish Christians because they did not worship Caesar. But Revelation 4–5, with their descriptions of the heavenly worship of Christ, reminded and encouraged Christians at that time that Jesus is Lord, not Caesar.

Revelation 6–18 predicts the coming judgments that Christ will dispense on Jerusalem for selling out Jewish Christians to Rome. The seal, trumpet, and bowl judgments depict divine judgment on Palestine during the Jewish revolt, especially from AD 66 to 70, through the hands of the Roman generals Vespasian and Titus. Thus the seal judgments unfold the Roman legions' destruction of Galilee (66–68), while the trumpet and bowl judgments (AD 69–70) depict Rome's turning up the heat on Palestine by defeating Judea and laying siege to Jerusalem. Revelation 17–18 predicts the fall of the "holy city" itself, the New Babylon!

Revelation 19 is a prediction of the actual coming of Christ to demolish Jerusalem in AD 70. Along the way, Revelation tells the two options Christians will have: either they can abandon their faith by worshiping Caesar, the beast, the Antichrist (Revelation 13; 16), or they can be faithful to Christ by refusing to worship Caesar (Revelation 7; 14). This last response is portrayed as the sealing or protecting of the 144,000. This number is a symbolic reference for the church, the true Israel, which has permanently replaced national Israel as the people of God, according to postmillennialists. We can come up with the number 144,000 as follows: 12 (tribes of Israel) times 12 (apostles) times 1000.

The former response (worshiping Caesar) leads to spiritual death, while the latter response (being faithful to Jesus) leads to eternal life.

But if Revelation 19 was fulfilled at the parousia (coming) of Christ to judge Jerusalem in AD 70, how does the millennium factor into this prophetic equation? After all, postmillennialism teaches that Christ will return *after* the millennium. So how is it that we can equate the time before AD 70 with the millennium? Revelation 20 provides the answer for the preterist.

Revelation 20 (21–22)

The postmillennial view begins its interpretation of Revelation 20 by stating two facts. First, Revelation 20 is the only passage in Scripture that speaks of a "millennium," a reign of Christ for a period of one thousand years. So the concept is rare, at best. Second, the millennium is a symbolic expression to be interpreted figuratively, which is in keeping with the symbolic nature of the book of Revelation. Indeed, one thousand is used symbolically of God's calculation of time: one thousand years before the eternal God is like only one day (Ps. 90:4; cf. 2 Peter 3:18).

Based on these two considerations, the postmillennial interpretation takes the millennium in Revelation 20 to be a figurative expression for the kingdom of God that appeared at Christ's first coming. This is the new covenant predicted by the prophets (Isaiah 40–66; Jeremiah 33; Ezekiel 36; Joel 2), which is realized in the church and has replaced the old covenant of Judaism.[10] With this understanding in mind, the postmillennialist reads Revelation 20 in the following way.

The millennium is John's symbolic portrayal of the kingdom of God, which came at the first coming of Christ. In that light, Revelation 20:1–3 is John's portrayal of the kingdom/millennium in negative terms: it meant the defeat and binding of Satan at the cross and resurrection of Jesus (cf. Matt. 12:28–29; John 12:30–33; Revelation 12). This allowed the first generation of Christians to preach the gospel beyond Israel so that the nations would no longer be deceived—that is, so that they could be converted to Christ. So the kingdom of God came with Jesus's life, death, and resurrection. It replaced the old covenant of Judaism with the new covenant of Christ, and it converted the Gentile nations.

Revelation 20:4–6 depicts the millennium/kingdom of God in positive terms. Since Satan was bound, Christ rules his redeemed people and they reign with him (v. 4). Those who died for Christ rule with him in heaven; those who are alive rule with Christ on earth. The "first resurrection" is spiritual in nature: it is the conversion of the sinner to Christ (John 5:24–29; Rom. 6:8; Eph. 2:1–10; Col 3:1–4).

At the end of the millennium, according to Revelation 20:7–15, Christ will again come to judge the world—especially unbelieving Jerusalem.

Evaluation of Biblical Postmillennialism

As creative and hopeful as the postmillennial view is, this school of thought can be criticized on several points.

First, as we mentioned in the last chapter, consistency dictates that the resurrections referred to in Revelation 20 are physical in nature, not just spiritual. Thus if the general physical resurrection of humanity is in view in Revelation 20:6–15 as almost all interpreters believe, then the first resurrection must be physical in nature. It is the resurrection of the martyred Christians to rule with Christ.

Second, the New Babylon in Revelation 17–18 is Rome and the Antichrist system it represents, not Jerusalem. Most interpreters agree, noting the undeniable connections in Revelation 17–18 with the seven hills of Rome, the ten first-century Roman caesars, and the unprecedented wealth of ancient Rome.

Third, when the Roman Empire is taken into consideration, the postmillennial reading of Revelation 19–20 breaks down in its argument that the millennium was a symbol for the rule of Christ through the triumph of the gospel over the nations. The Roman Empire ruled the world at that time, and not until AD 313 did Rome "fall" to the gospel, when Emperor Constantine legalized Christianity. Furthermore, Rome's persecutions of Christians during the first three centuries of the church are now infamous. How could one possibly say, then, that the millennium was the time between the first coming of Christ and his second coming to judge Jerusalem? This is one reason some postmillennialists have altered their view by arguing that the millennium did not begin until AD 313 (when Christianity was legalized) and that Christ did not return until he came to judge the city of Rome in the fifth century through the Barbarian hordes' several invasions of that city.

Fourth, Revelation 19:11–21 matches descriptions elsewhere in the New Testament that refer to the second coming of Christ in glory at the end of history (Matt. 24:30–31; Mark 13:26; Luke 21:27–28; 2 Thess. 2:8; Titus 2:13–14; Jude 14–15). Only with great difficulty can these texts be explained in terms other than the traditional understanding of the parousia, and they concur with Revelation 19:11–21.

Fifth, despite the preterist's attempt to root the *entirety* of the Olivet Discourse in history at the fall of Jerusalem, the best understanding of that tradition is to locate its ultimate fulfillment at the time of the return of Christ.[11] In our opinion, the preterist viewpoint makes a fundamental mistake in interpreting the Olivet Discourse by overlooking the parallel structure within it that itself is informed by the already/not-yet tension. This is especially clear in Luke 21, where the author distinguishes between the fall of Jerusalem in AD 70 (vv. 8–24) and the return of Christ at the end of history (vv. 25–36). That this chronological separation of the two events is intended by Luke is evidenced by two facts: (a) The fall of Jerusalem had already occurred by his day (see v. 20 and its specific description of that event, as contrasted with the generic presentations of Mark 13:14 and [possibly] Matt. 24:15); (b) Luke omits the phrase found in Mark 13:19 (cf. Matt. 24:21)—"those will be days of distress unequaled from the beginning . . . until now—and never to be equaled again"—with reference to the fall of Jerusalem. In other words, Luke did not equate the afflictions surrounding that event with the end tribulation. For Luke (and probably also Mark and Matthew, though less explicitly), the signs of the times already began at the fall of Jerusalem but will not be completed until the return of Christ to end world history.

Sixth, the preterist viewpoint makes much of the immediacy of the fulfillment of Jesus's promise in Revelation to come quickly, applying it to the fall of Jerusalem (Rev. 1:1, 3; 2:16; 3:11; 11:14; 22:6–7, 10, 12, 20). Put another way, the coming of Jesus Christ as recorded in 19:11–21 refers not to the second coming of Christ at the end of history but to the coming of Christ to judge Jerusalem in AD 70. But there is a major problem with this theory. The preterist interpretation does not take into account the nuance of the word "time" here (*kairos*, see Rev. 1:3), which is informed by the already/not-yet eschatological tension. This understanding, on the one hand, allows for the immediate fulfillment of the prophecy of Jesus in Revelation to come soon, while not denying, on the other hand, a future significance to those prophecies as well. That is to say the preterist position alleviates unnecessarily the tension between the already (the first coming of Jesus) and the not-yet (the second coming of Jesus). In effect, this viewpoint is akin to "realized eschatology," the view that says that basically all end-time prophecies of the New Testament were fulfilled in the first century, an interpretation rightly criticized.

Seventh, furthermore, a careful reading of Revelation 11 seems to indicate that God, even though having permitted the destruction of Jerusalem (see 11:1–2), is not yet finished with Israel/Jerusalem. We suggest that Revelation 11 is informed by the threefold paradigm operative in Romans 11, a pattern that envisions the future restoration of the Jewish nation. Romans 11 makes the basic point that God still has a plan for the Jews. Paul provides three arguments to that effect.

1. Israel's rejection of Jesus Messiah is partial, not total. Jewish Christians are ample testimony to that fact (11:1–12, where Elijah and Moses represent the Jewish Christian community at the end of history).
2. Israel's rejection of the Messiah serves a merciful purpose—it is the divine means for reaching Gentiles

with the gospel (11:11–29). This plan will be in effect until the end of history, at which time the fullness of the Gentiles will have arrived. The dominance of the Gentiles in the plan of God began with the destruction of Jerusalem in AD 70 (compare Rev. 11:2 with Luke 21:24) and will continue until God has accomplished his purpose with them (Rom. 11:25).

3. Israel's rejection of the Messiah is temporal, not eternal. One day Christ will return, and "all Israel will be saved" (11:25–36). At that culminating point, God will then restore Israel unto himself. This seems to be the sense behind Revelation 11:13. The seven thousand who will be killed in Jerusalem by an earthquake (a minority), leaving the rest of the city (the majority) to repent and turn to God, constitutes a *reversal* of the Elijah/remnant motif. In the Old Testament during Elijah's day, only he and the faithful seven thousand did not bow the knee to Baal, while the rest of the nation did. But in the end time, the opposite will take place—the witness of Elijah (and Moses, 11:3–12), along with the divine earthquake affirming their message (v. 13), will bring the majority of Jews to faith. This is John's apocalyptic way of saying what Paul had earlier said—"all Israel will be saved." That is, the nation as a whole will become the remnant, the ones who are faithful to God. Interestingly enough, the conversion of Jerusalem to Christ happens right before his second coming (11:15–19; cf. 19:11–21).

Eighth, all interpreters agree that Revelation 21–22, which follows John's description of the millennium in Revelation 20, describe the perfect eternal state of the new heaven and the new earth. The logical conclusion of the postmillennial interpretation is that, if the millennium occurred between AD 30 (the first coming of Jesus) and AD 70 (the second coming of Jesus to destroy Jerusalem), then from AD 70 until the present would have to correlate with the blissful eternal state.

But this is something that not even the postmillennialist would conclude! And even though the postmillennialists at this point just label all of this symbolic language and say it should be interpreted figuratively, their own reading of Revelation 19–22 dictates that the eternal state began in AD 70.

These eight criticisms of the biblical postmillennial/preterist school of thought are the reasons this viewpoint has never enjoyed the majority opinion among evangelical Christians; for that matter, neither has liberal postmillennialism, but for a different set of reasons we noted earlier in this chapter.

Conclusion

The postmillennial view has come under fire because most interpreters of the New Testament feel uncomfortable with overemphasizing the already aspect (thy kingdom came) to the exclusion of the not-yet aspect (thy kingdom come). Most interpreters prefer to read Revelation as predicting matters of end-time prophecies through the grid of the already/not-yet perspective. That is the subject of our next chapter.

4

Thy Kingdom Came/
Thy Kingdom Come

The Amillennial View of End-Time Prophecy

The members of the "greatest generation"—those who steered the ship of freedom called America between two world wars—well know the terms *D-day* and *V-day* as they applied to the Allied fight against Hitler and his forces. D-day was June 6, 1944, when the Allied forces—America, England, the French Resistance, and others—stormed the beaches of Normandy in France to take the battle to Hitler's Europe. It was a bloody, gruesome campaign that, thankfully, broke the back of the Nazi regime. D-day was the beginning of the end for the Third Reich, but still the horrors of war continued until the Allied forces prevailed over Nazi Germany in August 1945, V-day in Europe.

Oscar Cullmann, whom we met back in chapter 1, invoked the D-day/V-day events to illustrate the already/not-yet aspects of the kingdom of God. The first coming of Christ marked the arrival of the kingdom of God in its onslaught against the kingdom of Satan and this world. Jesus's message of righteousness and love, his miracles, atoning death, and bodily resurrection all signaled the dawning of God's rule in the hearts of his people. And yet, even though the kingdom of God is already here, it is not yet complete. Still the church encounters Satan who, like a snake with a broken back, continues to thrash out at the people of God through the venom of persecution. But when Jesus Christ returns at the end of human history, Satan will finally be banished and the church vindicated in the eternal state.

The reader will recall from chapter 1 Cullmann's already/not-yet interpretation of the kingdom of God/millennium/inaugurated eschatology. Other scholars saw things differently, however, notably Albert Schweitzer and C. H. Dodd. The first of these emphasized the not-yet aspect of the kingdom—the kingdom is not really here yet. This is called "consistent eschatology." This reminds one of the premillennial interpretation highlighted back in chapter 2 (though that viewpoint feels uncomfortable with the comparison with Schweitzer, the liberal theologian). C. H. Dodd taught just the opposite: the kingdom is fully here, the already aspect. This is called by scholars "realized eschatology," and it reminds one of the postmillennial interpretation just documented in chapter 3.

Cullmann's approach is most often associated with the amillennial interpretation—the kingdom is already here but not yet complete. This is the view I will focus on in this chapter.[1] To do so I will offer the following points: an explanation of amillennialism; a look at its hermeneutic, that is, what its principle of interpretation is; an overview of the amillennial interpretation of Revelation, especially Revelation 20; and a typical evaluation of this school of thought by those outside its camp.

Explanation of Amillennialism

The key Scripture in this discussion is Revelation 20. Amillennialists argue that the kingdom of God portrayed in Revelation 20 is spiritual in nature and therefore to be viewed figuratively. God's kingdom is intimately associated with the church, which between the first and second comings of Christ accomplishes God's will on earth; this despite the opposition the church encounters because it is in the midst of the end-time tribulation. For this school of thought, the binding of Satan in Revelation 20 for a short period of time corresponds to the present rule of Christ through the church until the parousia (vv. 1–4), which began at the cross/resurrection (John 12:31–33). The reference to the first resurrection is an allusion to Christians' conversion, at which time they began to reign with Christ (cf. Eph. 2:1–7; Col. 3:1–4). The reference to the battle of Gog and Magog anticipates the second coming of Christ, who at that time will finally defeat Satan and then establish the eternal state (Revelation 21–22). So in this configuration there will be no temporary, one-thousand-year reign of Jesus on earth between his parousia and the eternal state. The kingdom of God is here and now. Hence the name—"a- [no literal] millennium."

We will deal with Revelation 20 in more detail below. The following chart illustrates the amillennial interpretation of this Scripture:

Amillennialism

No future thousand–year reign of Christ

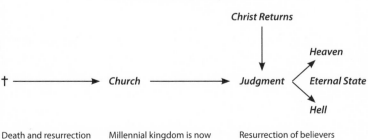

As to the worldview of this school of thought, "realism" is its preferred perspective. Stanley J. Grenz encapsulates this mind-set of the amillennial position:

> The result is a world view characterized by realism. Victory and defeat, success and failure, good and evil will co-exist until the end, amillennialism asserts. The future is neither a heightened continuation of the present nor an abrupt contradiction to it. The kingdom of God does not come by human cooperation with the divine power currently at work in the world, but neither is it simply the divine gift for which we can only wait expectantly.[2]

Consequently amillennialism declares that both unbridled optimism and despairing pessimism are inappropriate. Rather, the amillennialist worldview calls the church to "realistic activity" in the world. Under the guidance and empowerment of the Holy Spirit, the church will be successful in its mandate, yet ultimate success will come only through God's grace. The kingdom of God arrives as the divine action breaking into the world, but human cooperation brings important, albeit secondary, results. Therefore, God's people must expect great things in the present; while knowing that the kingdom will never arrive in its fullness in history, they must always remain realistic in their expectations.

The Hermeneutic of the Already/Not-Yet View of End-Time Prophecy "Tweaked" by Amillennialism

Hermeneutic means interpretation. It is well-known that the church throughout the centuries has interpreted the Bible in one of two ways: literally or allegorically. The first of these is the preferred approach. It takes the words of the Bible at face value, that is, it tries not to read something into the text that was not intended by the biblical author. Not that this approach eliminates figurative interpretation; it allows for such, but only when the text calls for it, for example, as the Psalms do.

The allegorical hermeneutic looks at the Bible much differently. An allegory is a story in which the details correspond to a deeper level of meaning than the literal sense. An allegory is a story that uses an extensive amount of symbolism, that is, most or many of the details in the story represent something or carry some specific nuance of meaning. Thus Bunyan's *Pilgrim Progress* is a well-known Christian book devoted to allegory. To understand it, one must read it figuratively and not as history. Some classic examples of allegory in the Bible include Isaiah 5:1–7 (Israel is the vineyard of God) and John 15:1–8 (Jesus as the vine and his followers as the branches). So allegory has its rightful place in Scripture.

However, allegory can be utilized in inappropriate ways, especially in regard to biblical prophecy. Sometimes narrative material in Scripture can be interpreted incorrectly in an allegorical manner instead of a more literal, historical manner, as the material was originally intended to be understood.

This method had its origin in Alexandria, Egypt, a Christian center of scholarship led by Clement of Alexandria in AD 190 and then by Origen in AD 200. The Alexandrian school was influenced by Platonic philosophy and understood the task of biblical interpretation as seeking the allegorical or symbolic meaning of the Bible, which lay behind the literal sense. While the motivation of this school of thought was laudable (it sought to show that the Old Testament is filled with messianic predictions now fulfilled in Jesus Christ), its methodology (reading the New Testament back into the Old Testament without the latter having any say in it) was incorrect. Regrettably, such an interpretation paved the way for later theologians to see Christ everywhere in the Old Testament, without regard for the intent of the inspired author. For example, the tabernacle as described in Exodus has been the breeding ground of fanciful messianic readings. Thus the tent pegs of the Holy Tent are thought to anticipate the cross of

79

Christ (never mind the fact that the tent pegs were *not* wood, but bronze, the latter of which is supposedly symbolic of our salvation in Christ that does not decay)! And the pins were buried in the ground but emerged from the ground when the tabernacle moved, thus bespeaking the death and resurrection of Christ. And on and on the messianic interpretation of the tabernacle goes. Now there is certainly a connection between the tabernacle and Christ, according to the book of Hebrews, but it is the general point that Christ is the superior replacement to the ancient holy tent, not the specific far-fetched details often teased from the Exodus narrative regarding the tabernacle.

Thus it is important to recognize that the interpreter today is not free to use allegorical methods to interpret Scripture whenever the interpreter feels as though it might be appropriate. It is critically important first to identify whether the biblical author intended the passage to be allegorical in nature. While allegories do occur in Scripture, as we have seen in the examples of Isaiah 5:1–7 and John 15:1–8, they are fairly rare, and today's interpreters should exert extreme caution before using the allegorical method to interpret most biblical texts. But the amillennial approach seems to throw such caution to the wind in the way it interprets end-time prophecy in general and the millennium in particular.

Now the already/not-yet approach follows the literal hermeneutic in its attempt to understand the New Testament's teaching on the kingdom of God. Thus it believes the kingdom of God arrived literally in the ministry of Jesus (see, for example, Mark 1:15; Luke 17:21) but the kingdom has not yet conquered the earth (Matt. 6:10). All of this is based on the near/far fulfillment dynamic discussed back in chapter 1.

But the already/not-yet eschatological tension takes on a different look in the hands of the allegorical hermeneutic in two ways. First, the kingdom of God will not be a literal rule of Christ on earth in the future; rather, it is Christ's reign through his church now. Put another way, the church has replaced Israel as the people of God. Second, the tribulation period should not be viewed as a future, literal seven-year outpouring of intense persecution on the people of God; rather, it is a symbolic concept that applies to the church now. This is what the not-yet aspect of the kingdom means to amillennialists—not that the kingdom is only partially here through the church but, rather, the kingdom is fully here in the church but it is still opposed by evil. We now unpack these two allegorical twists of the amillennial view.

The Church as the True Israel

Simply put, the Old Testament promises to Israel that God will give her a new covenant (Jeremiah 31; Ezekiel 36; Joel 2) and restore her to her land (Isaiah 40–66; Ezekiel 40–48; Daniel 11–12; Zechariah 12) are reapplied by amillennialists in a figurative way to the church. Thus Christ has established the new covenant with his followers, not the followers of Moses (see Matt. 26:26–30; Mark 14:22–26; Luke 22:14–20; 2 Corinthians 3–4; Hebrews 8). And the restoration of Israel to Palestine is reinterpreted as the spiritual rest that belongs to the church in Christ (see especially Heb. 3:7–4:13). For the amillennialist all of this is thought to be confirmed by those passages that call, or imply that, the church is the true Israel. Thus in the Gospels, the twelve apostles replace the twelve tribes of Israel. In Galatians 6:16 Paul calls the church "the Israel of God." In Romans 2:28–29 Paul implies that the church is spiritual Israel. Hebrews reinterprets the major institutions of Old Testament Israel (covenant, sacrifices, tabernacle, and others) as now devolved onto the church in Christ. In 1 Peter 2:5–10 names that were once applied to Israel are applied to the church—"spiritual house," "a royal priesthood," "a holy nation," and so on. And Revelation 7 and 14 reinterpret the church in terms of the twelve tribes of Israel.

Rolling these passages together, the amillennialist believes that the church has permanently replaced Israel as the people of God, and its citizenship is in heaven, not in geographical Palestine. Now, not surprisingly, premillennialists beg to differ with this "replacement theology" view. Rather, they say, the church has only temporarily replaced Israel in the plan of God, not permanently.

The two key passages amillennialists appeal to in support of their view are Romans 11 and Revelation 20. These are the two battleground texts in terms of the hermeneutical clash between premillennialists and amillennialists. We look at Romans 11 here and in the next section will focus on Revelation 20.

The reader will recall that premillennialists interpret "Israel" in Romans 11 as literal Israel, ethnic Jews who, as a nation, will come to Christ in the end times. Indeed, 1948 and the Jews' regathering to Palestine may have begun the fulfillment of that hope, according to some premillennialists. Amillennialists, however, do not read Romans 11 that way. In other words, they deny that Paul is predicting a future conversion of national Israel (though theoretically the amillennialist could subscribe to such a position, as long as it did not imply an actual millennial reign of Christ on earth.)[3] Therefore, the amillennialist counters the three points of the premillennialist reading of Revelation 11, that Israel's rejection is partial, merciful, and temporary.

ISRAEL'S REJECTION OF CHRIST

The amillennialist says that Israel rejected Christ and therefore God has replaced her with the church, which is composed of *both* Jewish Christians (Rom. 11:1–10) and Gentile Christians (Romans 9–10; cf. 2:28–29). In other words, the remnant of Israel, the elect, is the church—spiritual Israel *not* national Israel.

ONE PEOPLE OF GOD

God did use Israel's rejection of Christ for a merciful purpose, namely, to win Gentiles to Christ so they could form the one people of God (Rom. 11:11–24; cf. vv. 28–36). In other words, amillennialists reject the dispensational, pre-millennial notion that there are two peoples of God—Israel in the Old Testament, saved by the law of Moses, and the church in the New Testament, saved by the grace of Christ. Instead, amillennialists argue that there has always been only one people of God—those whose faith is in him.[4] Israel as a nation was a part of that people in the Old Testament but now is not because she has rejected the gospel of faith in Christ. Now the church (which was anticipated in the Old Testament) fulfills the function once held by Israel. And even though the church is composed of Christian Jews and Christian Gentiles, unbelieving ethnic Israel is no longer a part of the people of God.

PERMANENT REJECTION

The amillennialist believes that ethnic Israel's rejection of Christ is permanent not temporary. Israel's rejection of Jesus as Messiah will continue until the return of Christ (Rom. 11:25–27). So the "all Israel" that will be saved (v. 26) is the church, true Israel, not national Israel.

Thus, according to the amillennialist, Romans 11 holds out no hope for the future restoration of ethnic Israel, if restoration means the current State of Israel is going to convert to Christ in the end times. This amillennial approach of course also offers a totally different way of reading the book of Revelation, especially chapter 20, as I will discuss later in this chapter. But before dealing with that topic, we must look at how the amillennialist reinterprets the tribulation period.

Tribulation Here and Now

We discussed the end-time tribulation back in chapter 2 with regard to premillennialism. But here let us focus on it a little more carefully. Although Second Temple Jewish apocalypticism (ca. 200 BC to AD 100) was not a unified

83

movement, certain commonalities emerge in the writings, including the use of symbolism and visions; an emphasis on angelic mediators of revelation; the expectation of divine judgment; a fervent desire for the advent of the kingdom of God and, with it, the arrival of the new heavens and new earth; and the dualism of the two ages. The last of these similarities especially informs the concept of the messianic woes as found in this literature, where the suffering of this present age is portrayed as giving way to the glory of the age to come. The transition period between these two ages was expected to be accomplished by an intensification of affliction as it was perpetrated on godly Jews, and this, in turn, was expected to give birth to the messianic age, hence the phrase often used for the end-time tribulation: "the birth pangs of the Messiah" (see, for example, *1 Enoch* 52:4; *IQH* 3:7–18; Mark 13:8; 1 Thess. 5:3; Rev. 12:2–5) or "the messianic woes." The concept is hinted at in the Old Testament in association with the coming day of the Lord (see, for example, Isa. 24:17–23; Dan. 12:1–2; Joel 2:1–11, 28–32; Amos 5:16–20; Zeph. 1:14–2:3) and developed in Jewish apocalypticism (see, for example, *4 Ezra* 7:37; *Jub.* 23:11; 24:3; *2 Bar.* 55:6; *1 Enoch* 80:4–5). The term *messianic woes*, however, does not occur until the writing of the Talmud (see, for example, *b. Shab.* 118a; *b. Pes.* 118a [second to fifth centuries AD] in origin).

There is striking agreement in the literature under consideration regarding the appearance of the signs of the times, which will culminate in the arrival of the kingdom of God. Some six portents can be delineated:

1. *Earthquakes*—*As. Mos.* 10:41; *T. Levi* 4:1; *4 Ezra* 9:3; *2 Bar.* 2:7; *Apoc. Ab.* 30; cf. Mark 13:8; Matt. 24:7; Luke 21:11

2. *Intense famine*—*4 Ezra* 6:22; *2 Bar.* 27:6; 70:8; *Apoc. Ab.* 30; cf. *b. Sanh.* 97a; *b. Meg.* 17b; Mark 13:8; Matt. 24:7; Luke 21:11; Rev. 6:8; 18:8

3. *Wars*—*1 Enoch* 90; *4 Ezra* 6:24; *2 Bar.* 27:4; 48:32, 37; 70:3, 6, 8; cf. *b. Sanh.* 97a; *b. Meg.* 17b; Mark 13:8; Matt. 24:6; Luke 21:9; Rev. 6:4

4. *Internecine strife*—*1 Enoch* 100:1–2; 56:7; *4 Ezra* 6:24; *2 Bar.* 70:3–7; *m. Sota* 9:15; *b. Sanh.* 97a; cf. *Jub.* 23:16; Mark 13:12; Matt. 24:10; Luke 21:16

5. *Cosmic disturbances*—*Sib. Or.* III. 796–808; *1 Enoch* 80:4–6; *As. Mos.* 10:5–6; *4 Ezra* 5:4, 5; cf. with *B. Sanh.* 99a; Mark 13:24–25; Matt. 24:27; Luke 21:25; Rev. 6:12–14

6. *The persecution of God's people, which will sorely tempt them to depart from the faith*—Isa. 26:20–21; Jer. 30:4–9; Dan. 9:26–27; 11:36–12:1; Joel 2:20–31; Dead Sea Scrolls (1*QH*); Matt. 10:17–25; 24:10; Mark 13:9–13; Luke 21:12–17; John 15:18–16:4a

Now, whereas premillennialists believe the end-time tribulation period has not yet happened but will occur in the future seven years before the second coming of Christ, amillennialists believe that Jesus's first coming inaugurated not only the kingdom of God but also the messianic woes. This can be seen from two facts. First, the messianic woes were poured out on Jesus on the cross, but he arose victoriously over Satan, and, second, the signs of the times. Thus Dale C. Allison writes:

Jesus inaugurated the time of eschatological fulfillment (Mark 1:14–15). Especially noteworthy are the significant correlations between Mark 13 (about the end of the age) and Mark 14–15 (about the end of Jesus). Compare 15:33 (darkness at the crucifixion) with 13:24 (darkness at the end); 15:38 (the Temple veil torn) with 13:2 (the Temple will be destroyed); 14:34, 37 (Jesus tells his disciples to "watch" then comes and finds them sleeping) with 13:35–36 ("watch lest the master come and find you sleeping"); 14:10, 18, 21, 41 (Jesus is "delivered up") with 13:9 (the disciples will be "delivered up"); 14:53–65 (Jesus appears before a council of Jewish elders) with 13:9 (the disciples will appear before Jewish councils); 14:65 (Jesus is beaten) with 13:9 (the disciples will be beaten); 15:1–15 (Jesus before Pilate) with 13:9 (the disciples will stand before governors and kings). The meaning of these and other parallels, as well as of those between Mark 13 and Zechariah 9–14 (a little apocalypse) is plain; Jesus' end belongs to the eschatological drama.[5]

John 12:20–50, Jesus's discourse on his last hour on earth—his death and resurrection—broadens this picture in connecting eight end-time events with Jesus's passion. These eight aspects of "realized eschatology" are summarized here.

THE CONVERSION OF THE GENTILES: JOHN 12:20–23, 32

The Old Testament prophets prophesied that in the end times Gentiles will stream into Jerusalem to worship God (Isa. 45:15; 60:15–17; Zech. 8:20–23; Tobit 13:11). It is interesting in that regard to observe that in the account in John, the attempt of Gentiles to see Jesus prompts him to announce that his hour—his death and resurrection—has arrived (v. 23). In other words, the nations of the world were beginning to stream into Jerusalem to worship God through Christ. The "Greeks" referred to here may have come from the Decapolis area or even beyond Israel.

RESURRECTION: JOHN 12:23–26

Commentators connect John 5:19–30 with the end-time resurrection that began in Jesus's life and ministry. So also is the end-time resurrection of Jesus prophesied in John 12:23b–26, which specifies that Jesus's resurrection and glorification (v. 23b) will come because of his obedient suffering on the cross (v. 24). And those who want a share in his resurrection must also suffer with him (vv. 25–26; cf. Mark 8:34–38; Matt. 16:24–28; Luke 9:23–27). Thus Jesus's resurrection will inaugurate the breaking into history of the general resurrection of humanity.

THE MESSIANIC WOES: JOHN 12:28–30

As we saw above, much of Second Temple Judaism expected that Israel would undergo unprecedented affliction immediately before the Messiah comes (Dan. 12:1; *4 Ezra* 7:37; *Jub.* 23:11; *2 Bar.* 55:6; *1 Enoch* 80:4–5; 1QM). Jesus's reference in John 12:27 to his soul being troubled should be linked with John 15:18–16:4, a section devoted to describing the messianic woes that Jesus and his disciples undergo. But already in John 12:27 Jesus alludes to those eschatological sufferings which, of course, Revelation 6–19 deals with in greater detail.

We should also mention with the commentators that Jesus's remark in John 12:27 is reminiscent of Jesus's temptation in the Garden of Gethsemane (mentioned by the Synoptics but not John), when he asked that God would spare him from the cross. Jesus, however, submitted to God's will. According to John 12:28, God responded to Jesus's submission to his will by assuring his Son that just as he glorified Christ on earth through his miracles, so would he glorify Christ in his death and resurrection.

HOLY WAR: JOHN 12:31

Much of Second Temple Judaism expected that God's Messiah would appear at the end of the age to fight and defeat Satan (Ezekiel 38–39; Dan. 7:8, 25; 11:36, 40–41; 1QM; 1 John 4:3; Rev. 11:7, 13; 13:2, 5, 7). This is the backdrop for John 12:31. Jesus's death and resurrection would be the moment of the end-time holy war and the defeat of Satan, the prince and ruler of this world.

THE APPEARANCE OF THE MESSIAH/SON OF MAN: JOHN 12:33–34

That Jews in Jesus's day longed for the Davidic Messiah to appear at the end of the age and exalt Israel is clear in verse 34. And such a Messiah will reign on David's throne forever (cf. 2 Sam. 7:13; Pss. 61:6–7; 89:3–4, 35–37; Isa. 9:7; Ezek. 37:25;

Ps. Sol. 17:4; *Sib. Or* 3:49–50; *1 Enoch* 62:14; 4*QFlor.* 1:1–2:4). "Son of Man" was also a messianic figure in some Jewish texts (Dan. 7:13–14; *1 Enoch* 46:1; 47:3; *4 Ezra* 7:28–29; 13:32; 4Q246). Though it is debated by scholars, the crowd may well have assumed that the Messiah and the heavenly Son of Man refer to the same individual. If so, the crowd would have been surprised to hear Jesus speak of the suffering and death of the Messiah/Son of Man (v. 34).

DUALISM: JOHN 12:35–36

Jewish apocalypticism was famous for its temporal and ethical dualistic (either/or) categories. The former was expressed in terms of the opposition of the two ages: this age versus the age to come. The latter was expressed in terms of the contrast between the righteous and the wicked. Both of these aspects occur in the Dead Sea Scrolls, especially the *Community Rule* (1QS) 3:1–4:26. There the language of the sons of light versus the sons of darkness is strikingly similar to John 12:35–36 (cf. 1 John 1:5–7; 2:8–11; Rev. 21:23–25; 22:5). The sons of light in John's Gospel are those who believe in Jesus, while those who do not follow him remain in darkness.

APOSTASY: JOHN 12:37–43

Jewish apocalyptic literature also expected that in the end time many of the people of God would abandon the faith rather than face the persecution of the messianic woes (*Jub.* 23:14–23; *4 Ezra* 5:173; *1 Enoch* 90:3–10; cf. Matt. 24:10–13; Mark 13:20–23; Luke 21:34–36; 1 Tim. 4:1–5; 2 Tim. 3:1–5; Rev. 13:15–18). John 12:37–43 seems to apply that sign of the time to Jesus's audience. Such apostasy on their part was based on their rejection of Jesus the suffering servant. Isaiah predicted this long ago, and John quotes here from Isaiah 53:1 and 6:10. Compare verse 41 with Isaiah's call in 6:1–8. Pulling together the three Isaiah quotations here in John, we may say that the fourth evangelist declares that

Jesus the suffering, rejected servant was raised to glory. But despite Jesus's miracles (v. 37) and his fulfillment of Isaiah's prophecy (vv. 38–41), some of the Pharisees would not fully believe in him. This was end-time apostasy.

JUDGMENT DAY: JOHN 12:44–50

As is frequently noted by the commentators, end-time judgment in the fourth Gospel has become a present reality. One's response to Jesus now seals one's destiny: to believe in him is to receive eternal life now, to reject him is to receive condemnation now (vv. 46–50), for how people responded to Jesus is how they responded to God (vv. 44–45, 49–50).

It is clear in all of this that the end-time tribulation/messianic woes/signs of the times—or whatever we should call these eschatological events—are connected by the four Gospels with Jesus's death and resurrection. His death embraced the end-time tribulation, while his resurrection gave him victory over it.

Also the same end-time events of the tribulation are applied by the four Gospels to the disciples of Jesus and all later followers. Here we turn to John 15:18–16:4a, a passage remarkably similar to the Olivet Discourse of the Synoptic Gospels—Matthew, Mark, and Luke. Matthew 10:17–25 should also be factored into the mix. Raymond Brown has nicely charted the similarities between John 15:18–16:4a and the Olivet Discourse of the Synoptics.[6]

Parallels between John 15:18–16:4 and the Olivet Discourse

John xv 18—xvi 4a	Matt x 17–25, xxiv 9–10	Mark xiii 9–13; Luke xxi 12–17
xv 18: "The world hates you . . . has hated me before you"	x 22: "You will be hated by all because of my name"; also xxiv 9	Mark xiii 13; Luke xxi 17: same as Matthew
20: "No servant is more important than his master"	x 24: "No servant is above his master"	

89

John xv 18—xvi 4a	Matt x 17–25, xxiv 9–10	Mark xiii 9–13; Luke xxi 12–17
20: "They will persecute you"	x 23: "When they persecute you"; cf. also xxiii 34	Luke xxi 12: "They will persecute"
21: "They will do all these things to you because of my name"	See first parallel above	See first parallel above
26: "The Paraclete . . . will bear witness on my behalf"	x 20: "The Spirit of your Father speaking through you"	Mark xiii 11: "The Holy Spirit [speaking]"; cf. Luke xii 12
27: "You too should bear witness"	x 18: "You will be dragged before governors and kings . . . to bear witness"	Mark xiii 9; Luke xxi 12–13: almost the same as Matthew
xvi 1: "To prevent your faith from being shaken"	xxiv 10: "The faith of many will be shaken"	
2: "They are going to put you out of the Synagogue"	x 17: "They will flog you in their synagogues"	Mark xiii 9: "You will be beaten in synagogues"; Luke xxi 12: "Delivering you up to the synagogues"; cf. also Luke vi 22
2: "The man who puts you to death"	xxiv 9: "They will put you to death"	Mark xiii 12: "Children will rise against parents and will put them to death" (= Matt x 21); Luke xxi 16: "Some of you they will put to death"

It is clear from this that the end-time tribulation described in the Olivet Discourse is applied in the Gospel of John to the trials of Jesus's twelve disciples and all would-be followers. So, like Jesus, his followers also experience the messianic woes. The difference between Jesus and the disciples, however, is that the former overcame the tribulation at his resurrection, whereas the latter will have to continue to battle Satan and the signs of the times until the second coming of Christ at the end of history.

90

Thus the amillennial view asserts that the first coming of Christ "already" inaugurated the kingdom of God. But it is "not yet" completely triumphant because it battles Satan during the messianic woes and will continue do so until the return of Christ. Premillennialists, however, criticize the amillennialists for toning down the magnitude of the kingdom and the tribulation because they allegorize the details of these two realities.

Revelation (20)

Even more so than Romans 11, the book of Revelation, especially chapter 20, is the key battleground text in this discussion. For their part, amillennialists accept the label "allegorical" as their hermeneutic because they believe Revelation is a symbolical book through and through; thus it demands to be read figuratively. Therefore Raymond Calkins captures the chief message of Revelation in terms of five propositions:

1. It is an irresistible summons to heroic living.
2. It contains matchless appeals to endurance.
3. It tells us that evil is marked for overthrow *in the end*.
4. It gives us a new and wonderful picture of Christ.
5. It reveals to us the fact that history is in the mind of God and in the hand of Christ as the author and reviewer of the moral destinies of men.[7]

While all of the schools of interpretation surveyed here resonate with these affirmations, the idealist/amillennial view distinguishes itself by refusing to assign the preceding statements to any historical correspondence and thereby denies that the prophecies in Revelation are predictive, except in the most general sense of the promise of the ultimate triumph of good at the return of Christ. Thus the idealist/amillennialist does not restrict the contents of Revelation to a particular historical period but rather sees it as an apocalyptic dramatization of the continuous battle between God and evil. Because the symbols are multivalent and without specific historical referent, the application of the book's message is limitless. Each interpreter can therefore find significance for his or her respective situation.

Since the amillennialist believes Revelation speaks of the present tense of God's kingdom at work through his church in the world, and the tribulation as a current reality too, the only things that are still future in terms of end-time prophecy are the return of Christ at the end of history (Revelation 19; 20:7–15) and the new heaven and new earth (chaps. 21–22). Therefore the present tense is marked by the conflict between the kingdom of God and the tribulation. The clearest statement of the first of these is in Revelation 20:1–6. The binding of Satan took place at the cross and resurrection of Jesus. The first resurrection alludes to the conversion of the Christian and therefore is spiritual in nature. The saints' reign in Christ's kingdom began, then, at their conversion, when they were raised to the heavenlies and were seated on the divine throne with Christ. Things will continue that way until the second coming of Christ, which will make public his and his followers' invisible kingdom. Revelation 7 and 14 portray the same truth but use the numerical symbol of the sealing of the 144,000 for the church, the true Israel. The church, the replacement of Israel, reigns now with Christ on high (see 1:6).

In utter contrast to the preceding, while God's people are sealed and reign with him as priests, the wicked are judged by the seal, trumpet, and bowl judgments poured out on the earth. These judgments of God come in various forms: disease, catastrophes, wars, and so on. And their differing levels of intensity (seals—one-fourth of the earth; trumpets—one-third of the earth; bowls—whole earth) are a symbolic way of saying that God metes out judgment on nonbelievers in proportion to their evil deeds.

The Antichrist is any form of anti-God government in history: Roman Empire, Nazi Germany, Communist China, pagan

America, even the church if it abandons its testimony of Christ during times of persecution. But God always has a people for his name—the true church that is faithful to him.

Evaluation of the Amillennial Approach

What shall we say about this time-honored interpretation of the millennium, popularized by Augustine and championed by much of Christendom since then? On the positive side, amillennialism must be commended on at least four points.

1. Its already/not-yet construct has been embraced to some degree by every major eschatological school of thought—biblical and liberal postmillennialism, dispensational and historic premillennialism, even skeptical scholarship (see the next chapter for this viewpoint). The already/not-yet dynamic is what drove the New Testament authors.

2. The commitment to apply the message of Revelation and end-time prophecy to Christians and the world throughout church history is laudable and practical.

3. This application of end-time prophecy does not degenerate into seeing every current event as a sign of the end of history (as some dispensationalists are wont to do).

4. The realist philosophy of history that the amillennial viewpoint espouses is a healthy balance between the unbridled enthusiasm of the postmillennialist on the one hand and the dire pessimism of the premillennialist on the other hand. Thus the church can expect to encounter both triumph (the kingdom of God) and tribulation (the persecution from anti-God societies) through its earthly existence. That tribulation will culminate at the end of history in a final stand against the onslaught of evil. And Christ and his church will win in the end (Revelation 19–20).

On the negative side, the number one criticism of the amillennial perspective by both postmillennialists and premillennialists is its unfettered employ of the allegorical method of interpretation. Such an approach was born out of the Platonic dualism between the invisible but real world of ideas and the visible but nonreal world of copies. To the latter belongs the literal, surface reading of the text while to the former belongs the symbolic, deeper significance of that text. Thus Jewish exegesis was replaced by Platonic dualism. With Augustine, the church officially left behind its Jewish heritage, which read the Scriptures literally,[8] replacing it with Greek hermeneutics. But if the church would have followed the Jewish preference for the literal, normal method of reading a text (which the New Testament authors appear to do), then the church's teaching could have held on to both the already/not-yet tension and a future, temporal messianic kingdom on earth. Indeed, a number of amillennialists have come to admit this fact, especially the hope for the conversion of the nation of Israel.[9] The following chart encapsulates the Platonic influence on the allegorical reading of Scripture, from which amillennialists must distance themselves.

Idea	Copy
Invisible, real world	Visible, inferior, unreal shadows
Symbolic interpretation brings out the real meaning of the text.	Literal interpretation brings out only the superficial understanding of the text; therefore one must go behind this reading to get to the symbolic, true meaning of the text.

Conclusion

It is time now to take a step back and survey the lay of the land of the three major schools of interpretation of end-time prophecy and the millennium that we have summarized thus far.

There is, I believe, truth in each of the three major schools of interpretation. I agree with the amillennialist that the kingdom already came at the first coming of Christ but will not triumph until his second coming at the end of history as we know it. And like the postmillennialist, I suspect the fall of Jerusalem to the Romans formed a significant part of the background of the New Testament, but this does not rule out a return of Christ at the end of history. Recall my comments in chapter 3 to that effect. Yet, agreeing with the premillennial perspective, I see no reason to deny a future, temporary reign of Christ on earth immediately following his return. Taking seriously the early church's indebtedness to Jewish exegesis leads me to this conclusion.

It must be said in all of this that all three major schools of interpretation of eschatology—premillennialism, postmillennialism, and amillennialism—are rooted in conservative convictions. And each group should of course show love and respect for their colleagues across the evangelical spectrum regarding this issue. There is a large, formidable group of interpreters, however, who debunk the Bible and end-time prophecy. They offer the skeptical view of the kingdom of God. To that influential view we now turn.

5

Thy Kingdom Did *Not* Come

The Skeptical View of End-Time Prophecy

The reverent reader of biblical prophecy is in for a surprise in this chapter on the skeptical view of New Testament eschatology, for many today are no longer enamored with the events surrounding the return of Christ, the millennium, or even heaven itself. Rather, the skeptics we will meet in this chapter decry biblical prophecy, believing it to be a man-made system born out of superstition and designed to be used as a scare tactic to control the masses. But it behooves the Christian to know something about these radical ideas so as not to let them steal from the Christian the joy of end-time prophecy.

The quests for the historical Jesus, *The Da Vinci Code*, the Jesus Seminar—stretching across the twentieth century into our own day, in their own ways these are all attempts to debunk end-time prophecy. And they claim millions of followers, whose skeptical view of the kingdom of God is giving traditional Christianity a run for its money! Therefore these skeptical approaches require a rebuttal from those of us who love end-time prophecy, who cherish the inspiration of the Bible, and who are not ashamed to stand for the exclusive claim of the New Testament—that Jesus Christ is the Messiah and the only way to know God!

This chapter considers how nonevangelicals typically interpret end-time prophecy. We will do this by analyzing the three quests for the historical Jesus and the kingdom of God. These skeptical views are essentially antisupernatural in perspective. Thus, for example, the Jesus Seminar's *Five Gospels* "translation" (see below) begins with the following dedication:

> This report is dedicated to
> Galileo Galilei
> who altered our view of the heavens forever
> Thomas Jefferson
> who took scissors and paste to the gospels
> David Friedrich Strauss
> who pioneered the quest of the historical Jesus

The other movements we will track in this chapter are of the same piece of cloth in their antisupernatural biases. We turn now to a summary of the skeptical quests for the historical Jesus and the jettisoning of the idea of the kingdom of God.

From 1778 until the present day, a storm has been unleashed on traditional Christianity. Such a theological tempest has resulted in the quests for the historical Jesus, the label most often applied to this radical movement among New Testament scholars. This storm has unfolded in three stages, which are called the first quest for the historical Jesus, the second quest for the historical Jesus, and the third quest for the historical Jesus. The methods of those on the quest may differ but their agenda is the same: to deny that the Gospels give us a historically reliable picture of Jesus.

This chapter provides surveys of each of these three quests, providing an evangelical critique of them as well.

The Apocalyptic Jesus: The First Quest
for the Historical Jesus (1778–1906)

The radical assumption that the Gospels are not historically reliable documents but are later writings about Jesus that do not square with what he really said and did began with the appearance of the pamphlet *On the Intention of Jesus and His Disciples.* The work was written by H. Samuel Reimarus and published posthumously in 1778. As its title might suggest, two claims are made by Reimarus. First, Jesus was an end-time/apocalyptic preacher whose expectation of the soon arrival of the kingdom of God met with great disappointment. Second, in the wake of Jesus's death and the nonappearance of the kingdom, the disciples falsely claimed that Jesus was resurrected and that he would soon come again to establish his reign on earth.

The pamphlet created a firestorm of response from both its critics and adherents. These responses took on a life of their own, with the result that each New Testament scholar read his own opinion into the four Gospels. Some, like F. D. E. Schleiermacher, David F. Strauss (mentioned in the dedication above), and J. Ernest Renan, denied all elements of the supernatural in the four Gospels—excising Jesus's deity and miraculous works from the record. Others were no less benign in their reconstruction of the historical Jesus. Thus A. Harnack attracted a whole band of followers who reduced Jesus's life and death to mere moral, ethical teachings. Thereby the kingdom of God was scaled down to simply loving others. The conservative response of men like J. J. Hess to the radicals was well intentioned but not high powered enough academically to compete with the heavyweight theologians of the left wing.

But that stage of the quest for the historical Jesus came to a crashing halt with the publication of Albert Schweitzer's classic work in 1906, *The Quest of the Historical Jesus.* In his book Schweitzer masterfully demonstrated that the quest

99

for the historical Jesus amounted to nothing more than each interpreter imposing his own opinion of who Jesus really was onto the four Gospels. The result was a welter of conflicting offerings of the historical Jesus. As they looked into the waters of the Gospels, what interpreters saw was merely their own reflection: the devotional Jesus, the liberal Jesus, the ethical Jesus, and so on.

For Schweitzer's part, he sided with the position of Reimarus, the view that got the whole quest started in the first place. "Consistent eschatology" is a label that New Testament scholars applied to the works of Albert Schweitzer. "Consistent" means futurist, with reference to how Schweitzer interpreted the message of Jesus. As we have seen, Judaism at the time of Christ divided history into two periods: this age of sin, when sin rules, and the age to come, when the Messiah is expected to bring the kingdom of God to earth. Schweitzer concluded that an apocalyptic understanding of the kingdom was foundational not only for Christ's teaching but also to understanding his life. Thus Schweitzer maintained that Jesus believed it was his vocation to become the coming Son of Man. Initially Jesus revealed this messianic secret only to Peter, James, and John. Later Peter told it to the rest of the Twelve. Judas told the secret to the Jewish high priest, who used it as the ground for Jesus's execution (Mark 14:61–64; cf. Dan. 7:13).

According to Schweitzer's interpretation, when Jesus sent out the Twelve on a mission to proclaim the coming kingdom of God, he did not expect them to return. The Twelve were the men of violence who would provoke the messianic tribulation that would herald the kingdom (see Matt. 11:12). Whereas some earlier scholars believed that one could only wait passively for the kingdom, Schweitzer believed that the mission of Jesus was designed to provoke its coming. When this did not happen, Jesus determined to give his own life as a ransom for many (Mark 10:45), and this would cause the kingdom to come.

So, Schweitzer said, Jesus took matters into his own hands by precipitating his death, hoping this would be the catalyst for causing God to make the wheel of history turn to its climax—the arrival of the kingdom of God. But, said Schweitzer, Jesus was wrong again and he died in despair. So, for Schweitzer, Jesus never witnessed the dawning of the age to come; it lay in the distant future, separated from this present age.

According to Schweitzer, however, the apostle Paul put a new spin on the message of the historical Jesus. In his book *The Mysticism of Paul the Apostle*, Schweitzer argued that Paul's teaching rested on Jesus's proclamation that the kingdom of God was at hand. While for Jesus this kingdom was still future, Paul faced a new situation: if Christ's resurrection was the beginning of the age to come, why had the other events associated with the end of history (resurrection of righteous believers, judgment of the wicked, and so on) not also happened?

Schweitzer's proposed solution to this quandary was Christ-mysticism. Schweitzer argued that the Pauline phrase "in Christ" signifies that the kingdom of God or age to come has begun. But this is for Christians only because, through union with the Spirit, they have died and been raised with Christ. Schweitzer writes that through Christ we are moved out of this world and transferred into a state of existence proper to the kingdom of God, notwithstanding the fact that it has not yet appeared. In other words, Paul's Christ-mysticism was a makeshift attempt to explain how it was that, despite Jesus's resurrection, the kingdom of God had not yet appeared on earth.

Most scholars today give due credit to Schweitzer for demonstrating conclusively that Jesus was indeed an apocalyptic preacher. Conservative Gospel scholars, however, beg to disagree with Schweitzer's "consistent" view of Jesus and the kingdom. Rather, they side with Oscar Cullmann that "inaugurated eschatology" is the more accurate (and reverent!)

view of Jesus and the kingdom. Thus the kingdom of God did indeed arrive in Jesus's life, death, and resurrection. But it is not yet complete, awaiting the return of Christ.

Against Schweitzer, Paul's view of the kingdom also best fits with Cullmann's inaugurated eschatology. Note, for example, how the already/not-yet tension informs Paul's use of the phrases "kingdom of God" or "kingdom of Christ."

Text	Kingdom Description	Verb Tense
Rom. 14:17	Kingdom of God	Present tense
1 Cor. 4:20	Kingdom of God	Present tense
1 Cor. 6:9–10	Kingdom of God (twice)	Future tense
1 Cor. 15:24	Kingdom of Christ/ God (implied)	Future tense
1 Cor. 15:50	Kingdom of God	Future tense (implied in "inherit")
Gal. 5:21	Kingdom of God	Future tense
Eph. 5:5	Kingdom of Christ/ God	Future tense (implied in "inheritance")
Col. 1:13	Kingdom of Christ	Present tense
Col. 4:11	Kingdom of God	Present tense
1 Thess. 2:12	Kingdom of God	Present tense
2 Thess. 1:5	Kingdom of God	Future tense

Three observations emerge from the chart:

1. The kingdom of Christ/God is both present and future, already here and not yet complete. This is consistent with what is in the Gospels and Acts.
2. Christ and God are, in at least two instances, interchanged, suggesting equality of status between them (compare Eph. 5:5 with Rev. 11:15 and 12:10).
3. The most precise description of the exact relationship between the kingdoms of Christ and of God is found in 1 Corinthians 15:24—the interim messianic kingdom begun at the resurrection of Christ will one day give

way to the eternal kingdom of God. Such a temporary kingdom is attested to in apocalyptic Judaism and may be the background for Revelation 20:1–6. For Paul, then, the order of history would be as follows:

This age → temporary messianic kingdom → the age to come (kingdom of God)

Christians therefore live between the two ages, in the messianic kingdom. Recall the comments on this in chapter 2 on premillennialism.

The Form Critic: The Second Quest for the Historical Jesus (1920s to 1980s)

The second quest for the historical Jesus came in two waves: Rudolf Bultmann's form criticism and the Jesus Seminar's *Five Gospels*.

Rudolf Bultmann's Form Criticism

New Testament studies on Jesus took a different turn between the 1920s and the 1980s, though it was still a radical road they traveled. It was the road called "form criticism." Championed by Rudolf Bultmann in the 1920s through the 1960s and then popularized by the Jesus Seminar in the 1980s, form criticism continued the skeptical view of the historical reliability of the four Gospels regarding Jesus. The upshot of its approach was to drive a wedge between the Jesus of history and the Christ of faith. The former was thought to be the real Jesus, who has been lost amid the legendary portrayals found in the four Gospels. The latter—the Christ of faith—is the theological spin the early church put on Jesus, attributing miracles and sayings to him that he did not, in fact, perform or say. In other words, the church turned Jesus

103

into the Messiah and turned a mere mortal into God when he was neither Messiah nor God.

The movement started by Bultmann—a radical German theologian—was called form criticism because it divided the major types or forms in the four Gospels into two categories and subcategories. Thus:

Sayings of Jesus	Miracles of Jesus
parables	nature miracles
"I" sayings	healings and exorcisms
conflict stories	legends
apocalyptic statements	

In the first category—sayings of Jesus—the parables comprise some one-third of Jesus's teaching and have to do with the kingdom of God. "I" sayings refer to statements Jesus made identifying himself with the Messiah, Son of Man, or Son of God. The conflict stories portray Jesus in conflict with the Jewish leadership of his day. But Jesus ends the discussion with his critics time after time with a pronouncement, a "gotcha!" saying. And the apocalyptic statements refer to Jesus's postresurrection, future return to clean house on the earth for the sake of righteousness.

The miracles consist of supernatural feats by Jesus dealing with nature—walking on water, calming the storm, and so on—as well as healings of people, exorcisms of demons, and even raising people from the dead. The legendary miracles were once nonsupernatural things Jesus did that got embellished with each new telling—his wilderness temptations, the Holy Spirit descending on Jesus at his baptism in the form of a dove, and so on.

While recognizing that the Gospels, like any other portion of Scripture, contain different types or forms of literature that bring their own hermeneutical rules to the table is actually helpful, in the hands of Bultmann and his radical followers, form criticism went south in a hurry. Its assumption that most of what the Gospels purport that Jesus said and did, *did not* happen (the Jesus of history) but rather are fabrications of the church (the Christ of faith) leaves little confidence in the Gospels. In fact Bultmann and his followers didn't even think Matthew, Mark, Luke, and John wrote the Gospels that are attributed to them. Rather, later anonymous authors penned the Gospels under their names!

In 1953 Ernst Käsemann, a theologian trained by Bultmann, delivered the paper "The Problem of the Historical Jesus," in which he debunked Bultmann the debunker! In that paper Käsemann turned on his former professor, accusing his form critical method of being a dead-end street for the interpretation of the historical Jesus. Käsemann called for a return to a basic trust in the four Gospels' presentations; that is, the Jesus of history is essentially the Christ of faith.

Unfortunately, Käsemann did not stem the tide; after stepping out of the picture in the 1960s and 1970s, form criticism came back with a vengeance, this time in America, under the auspices of the Jesus Seminar.

The Jesus Seminar's Five Gospels: 1980s to the Present

The Jesus Seminar is a group of radical Gospel scholars who began meeting in 1985 for the purpose of color coding the four Gospels, which is actually a parody of the red-letter editions of the Gospels (red being the color of Jesus's words in the four Gospels to help distinguish them from the narrator's words in black).[1] The Fellows (the name of the members of the Jesus Seminar) put a whole new radical twist on color-coding the Gospels. The Fellows arrived at their color-coded translation via the American way. They voted on whether or not the five hundred references comprising Jesus's words and works in the four canonical Gospels were authentic, meaning actually spoken and performed by Jesus. The vote on each saying and act went basically like this:

> a red bead to indicate "Jesus surely said or did this"
> a pink bead for "Jesus probably said or did this"

105

a gray bead for "he probably didn't say or do that"
a black bead for "it's very unlikely that Jesus said or
did that"

What were the Fellows' final results? Only 18 percent of Jesus's sayings and acts in the Gospels were deemed authentic and colored red in their publications *The Five Gospels* and *The Acts of Jesus*![2] What criteria did the Fellows use to determine what Jesus genuinely said and did? Two assumptions—technical sounding but really very simple—guided them in their decision making. They used the criterion of dissimilarity and the criterion of multiple attestation. Let's begin by defining these terms.

The *criterion of dissimilarity* states that a Jesus saying or deed that stands out both from his Jewish heritage and from his later followers (the church) truly goes back to Jesus. In other words, the saying or deed has to be unique, thus dissimilar, from Jesus's Jewish culture or what his followers would say or do. The saying or deed only "counts" if it is in opposition to both groups.

The *criterion of multiple attestation* assumes there are four separate sources that make up the Gospels: Mark, Q (sayings of Jesus not in Mark but in Matthew and Luke), M (material only in Matthew), and L (material only in Luke). They omit John from the discussion (see the comment about John in the quote below). If a saying or deed attributed to Jesus occurs in two or more of these sources, it is thought to be authentic. If it occurs in only one source, it is not thought to be attested to and therefore is not considered authentic. When all is said and done, what is left of the Gospels as a result of this approach? Michael J. Wilkins and J. P. Moreland leave us in no doubt:

> In the entire Gospel of Mark, there is only one red-letter verse: "Give to Caesar what is Caesar's and to God what is God's" (Mark 12:17). Only fifteen sayings (not counting parallels) are colored red in all of the Gospels put together, and they are all

short, pithy "aphorisms" (unconventional proverb-like sayings) or parables (particularly the more "subversive" ones). Examples of the former include Jesus' commands to turn the other cheek (Matt. 5:39; Luke 6:29) and love your enemies (Matt. 5:44; Luke 6:27), and his blessing on the poor (Luke 6:20; *Thos.* 54). Examples of the latter include the parables of the good Samaritan (Luke 10:30–35), the shrewd manager (Luke 16:1–8a), and the vineyard laborers (Matt. 20:1–15). Seventy-five different sayings are colored pink, while at the other end of the color spectrum, several hundred appear in black, including virtually the entire Gospel of John and all of Jesus' claims about himself (e.g. "I am the way and the truth and the life"—John 14:6; "I and the Father are one"—10:30; and so on).[3]

So what portrait of Jesus emerges from the above "findings" of the Jesus Seminar? When the preceding two criteria, especially the principle of dissimilarity, are applied to Jesus, he ends up with no connection to his Jewish heritage and no ties to the church he founded. In other words, the Jesus Seminar portrays Jesus as a "talking head" with no body.

So this "talking head" Jesus appears to be nothing more than a Greek-style philosopher who utters mere moral maxims about how to treat each other, but who makes no claim to be the Messiah, announces no kingdom of God, makes no proclamation against sin, and subverts no religious establishment. One wonders in all of this, however, why was *this* Jesus ever crucified? The Jesus of the seminar might have ruffled some feathers among his fellow Jews, but he would not have undermined their core beliefs.

By now you will probably be aware that the Fellows' translation of the sayings and acts of Jesus is driven by their agenda to reinvent Jesus for the modern world. Two biases are driving this agenda: historical skepticism and political correctness.

HISTORICAL SKEPTICISM

The Jesus Seminar makes no bones about being skeptical of the reliability of the Bible in general and of the Gospels in particular. They express such suspicion in the "Seven Pillars of Scholarly Wisdom," which forms the introduction to their two books. What are these "seven pillars"?

1. The Jesus of history (the real Jesus who walked this earth) is *not* the Christ of faith (the Jesus of the four Gospels and the church).
2. The Jesus of the Synoptic Gospels (Matthew, Mark, and Luke) is not the same as the Jesus of the Gospel of John.
3. The Gospel of Mark was the first Gospel to be written (about AD 64–68), while Luke (AD 80) and Matthew (AD 90) relied on Mark in their portrait of Jesus.
4. The Q document (*Quelle*—German for source) refers to some 235 purported statements by Jesus; it was also used by Luke and Matthew.
5. Jesus was not a fiery Jewish preacher of the in-breaking kingdom of God (as Albert Schweitzer said) but rather a Greek philosopher–type who went around Palestine uttering proverbial niceties about the need for people to treat each other with equality.
6. The written Gospels of the New Testament were pieced together from oral tradition that had circulated in the churches a generation earlier, which attracted legends and myths after each retelling (that is, elements of the supernatural).
7. The burden of proof that the Jesus of history is the Christ of faith now rests squarely on conservative Christians. It is they who are under the gun to demonstrate the historical reliability of the Gospels.

Are the Fellows' "scientific findings" and "assured results" (as they would refer to them) indeed foolproof? The following examination will demonstrate otherwise. I will respond to the seven pillars in order.

First, is the Jesus of history different from the Christ of faith? The heart of this issue is the question of the reliability of the Gospels. Millions of Christians and thousands of theologians for the past two millennia have said yes to the dependability of the Gospels. Consider these facts:

1. The New Testament Gospel authors were either eyewitnesses to the historical Jesus or close associates of those who were. Thus Mark relied on the apostle Peter to write his Gospel; Matthew was one of the twelve disciples; John was the "beloved" disciple; and Luke wrote under the direction of Paul, who encountered the risen Jesus several times.

2. The four canonical Gospels report the same basic story line: Jesus was baptized by John the Baptist, claimed to be the Messiah, declared the kingdom of God had come in his person, began his ministry in Galilee, confronted Jewish and Roman authorities, was tried and crucified by the same but arose on the third day after his death, after which he was seen by some of those very ones who would later write the four Gospels.

3. The above basic story line is confirmed by Jewish and Roman writers outside the New Testament who lived in or shortly after the first century AD. Even though their remarks about Jesus and the early church are polemical in nature, they inadvertently confirm the story line found in the canonical Gospels.

Second, are the Jesus of the Synoptic Gospels (Matthew, Mark, and Luke) and the Jesus of the Gospel of John contradictory? No, for as the first point above noted, the four Gospels follow the same basic story line. Furthermore, it is now recognized by many biblical scholars that the Gospel of John adds supplemental material to the Synoptics' presentation of Jesus, for example, the seven sign miracles, the seven "I am" statements, and the upper room discourse. In addition, the passion narrative in John is similar to Luke's presentation.

Responding to the third and fourth pillars, many conservative biblical scholars do accept that Mark was the first Gospel written, and Matthew and Luke used Mark and a different source (Q) for sayings of Jesus to compose their Gospels. But this need not suggest that the Gospels are unreliable, especially if Mark wrote his Gospel under the auspices of Peter, and Matthew was the author of Q. What we have in that case is one writer building on an apostle's testimony—Mark using Peter, Luke using Matthew.

Fifth, if there is any assured scholarly result (what the Fellows were seeking) today in Gospel studies, it is that Jesus was indeed an apocalyptic preacher who believed that the kingdom of God was breaking into history through his messianic ministry (see Matt. 6:9–13; Mark 1:15; 4:1–41; 9:1; Luke 11:1–4; 17:20–21). Albert Schweitzer demonstrated this in the early twentieth century, and it has now become a near consensus among New Testament experts. Since the Fellows believed Jesus was a quiet Greek philosopher–type, there is little wonder that the first instance of Jesus's mention of the presence of the kingdom of God, in Mark 1:15—"The kingdom of God is near. Repent and believe the good news!" (NIV)—and all subsequent references to the kingdom of God in the other Gospels are in black in *The Five Gospels*! To admit this to be an authentic saying of Jesus would undermine the whole enterprise of the Jesus Seminar! They refuse to admit that Jesus is the heavenly Son of Man who calls for an end to this world as we know it.

Sixth, did the story of Jesus as passed on by word of mouth by the first Christians look much different by the time the second generation of Christians wrote it down? That is, were myths and legends added with each retelling of the story of Jesus? The answer is no, for a number of reasons:

1. The Jesus Seminar Fellows, like some liberal German theologians before them, assumed that the sayings and

deeds of Jesus were passed along in oral form in the same way the Grimm brothers' fairy tales were handed down—over hundreds of years, with each new telling embellishing the account with more dramatic flair. They thought of it like the kids' game "telephone," in which one child whispers a secret to the next, who whispers it to the next child, until the oft-told secret reaches the last person, who reveals a secret that bears little resemblance to the original. More recent biblical scholars recognize that this idea foists a Western mind-set on the Gospels, which were, after all, ancient Jewish Christian writings. That is to say, Jewish culture was adept at passing along accurate information in oral form, even as large blocks of African cultures do today.

2. The disciples, who were eyewitnesses to the historical Jesus, lived into the second generation of Christians. They were the gatekeepers of the "Jesus tradition," ensuring it was faithfully passed on. The only way the early church could have been free to tamper with the words and deeds of Jesus was if the apostles had died and gone to heaven with Jesus (assuming the early church wanted to do so in the first place).

3. Jesus promised that he would send the Holy Spirit to remind the disciples of what Jesus said and did precisely to make sure they got his story right (John 14:25–26). This last point won't convince the skeptic of the reliability of the Gospels, but for the believer today Jesus's promise that his apostles would be inspired by the Spirit as they passed along the memoirs of their Messiah is a reassuring word.

4. Thirty or so years between the time of Jesus and the writing of the Gospels is not much time for myths and legends to have been added to the Gospels. Not only that, but Paul's story of Jesus, which jibes with the story of Jesus as found in the Gospels, was written less

than fifteen years after Jesus's resurrection (see 1 Cor. 15:3–11; Gal. 3:1).

Responding to the seventh pillar, Christians have no problem accepting the burden of proof when it comes to substantiating the reliability of the Gospels. Bring it on! More than one skeptic who started out to disprove the Gospels has become a follower of Jesus. There's Frank Morrison, Josh McDowell, and Lee Strobel, to name only a few. Ironically, even Germany, home of much biblical skepticism in the past, in part has done an about-face on the subject, as the writings of Ernst Käsemann and Martin Hengel demonstrate. These scholars cannot be accused of being conservatives, yet their research again and again has confirmed the Gospels' reliability.

POLITICAL CORRECTNESS

The second bias of the Jesus Seminar I wish to expose is their desire to offer us a politically correct Jesus. Not that being politically correct is wrong. But it is incorrect to read a North American mentality back into the first-century Gospels. This becomes clear when one realizes that the Jesus Seminar places the *Gospel of Thomas* alongside the canonical Gospels, even according it priority over them. The *Gospel of Thomas* is a second-century AD Gnostic reinterpretation of Jesus. The Gnostics were a group of Christians who were considered heretical by the mainstream church; akin to the Greek philosopher Plato, they taught that the human body is evil and only the soul is good. According to them, in the beginning there was one cosmic spirit-being and no matter. But an evil creator god turned from the one true God and created the world. Gnostics believed that they were not of this world but descendants of the one true God. They thought of themselves as sparks of divine light entrapped by the evil creator god in the material world of his creation. Their goal—their salvation—was to escape this world and reascend to the heavenly realm of their origin.

112

In Christian Gnosticism, the redeemer figure was identified with Christ. He comes, as in other Gnostic systems, to remind Gnostics of their true nature, to awaken them from forgetfulness, and to tell them of their heavenly home. This Christ shares with them secret knowledge—gnosis—which is the means by which they can escape the world of evil and return to God.

The *Gospel of Thomas* reflects the outlook of the Gnostic movement in significant aspects. Jesus, for example, speaks as the redeemer come from God. He reminds his followers of humanity's forgetfulness and tells how it is in need of enlightenment (*Thomas* 28). He deprecates the world (21:6; 27:1; 56:1–2; 80:1–2; 110; 111:3). He reminds people of their origin (49) and tells them of their needed return to the heavenly home (50). He also speaks of his own return to the place from which he has come (38)

In addition, the *Gospel of Thomas* is individualistic—each person follows his or her own innate intuition, because that intuition is divine. That's how they follow Jesus. Thus saying 49 reads, "Blessed are the solitary and the elect, for you will find the Kingdom. For you came forth from it, and you will return to it." In other words, Thomistic "Christians" possess individually the true knowledge of their origin. Related to this, saying 70 reads, "Jesus said: If you gained this [truth] within you, what you have will save you. If you do have this in you, what you do not have in you will kill you." So Thomistic "Christians" understand that the truth is within them, namely, their origin is heaven, not earth, and it is this knowledge that will save them.

Thomas is also pantheistic—God is in the material universe, the spark of divine in humans. Saying 77 makes this clear: "Jesus said: I am the light that is above them all. I am the all; the all came from me, and the all attained to me. Cleave a [piece of] wood, I am there. Raise up a stone, and you will find me there."[4]

Furthermore, the *Gospel of Thomas* consists of 114 purported sayings of Jesus—with no passion narrative: Jesus does not die for sin and his body is not resurrected. In other words, this apocryphal work is moralistic in orientation. One is saved by following the light within, not by revelation from God from without.

The Jesus Seminar appeals to the *Gospel of Thomas* to prove that early Christianity was pluralistic. That is, they say that some Christians followed the four New Testament Gospels and others followed the Gnostic *Gospel of Thomas*. The Fellows are pleased to find that early Christianity was tolerant of alternative types of Christian faith. They see the Council of Nicea in Asia Minor (Turkey) in AD 325 as the turning point, when the orthodox view won out over the Gnostic approach and wrongly branded the latter heretical.

The Jesus Seminar makes quite an opening statement in its two books: "Beware of finding a Jesus entirely congenial to you." The ironic thing about this comment is that the Jesus Seminar has found in the five "Gospels" precisely the picture of Jesus they wanted to find—an individualistic, pantheistic, moralistic, pluralistic, North American Jesus!

Critiquing the Methods Used by the Fellows

Robert Funk is the guru of the Jesus Seminar. His forceful presence and drive formed a publishing group that in turn was responsible for producing *The Five Gospels* and *The Acts of Jesus*. Funk, like Rudolf Bultmann, ardently believes that there are two criteria for determining whether purported words and acts of Jesus are genuine: the criteria of dissimilarity and multiple attestation, discovered above. What about these two criteria? Do they have merit?

CRITERION OF DISSIMILARITY

Remember that this guideline says that for something to be authentically attributed to Jesus, it has to be different from both ancient Judaism and the practices of the early church, but there are at least two problems with this procedure. First, it is logically absurd. Darrell L. Bock expresses this criticism well:

> If both sides of the dissimilarity are affirmed, so that Jesus differs from *both* Judaism *and* the early church, then Jesus becomes a decidedly odd figure, totally detached from his cultural heritage *and* ideologically estranged from the movement he is responsible for founding. One wonders how he ever came to be taken seriously. He becomes an eccentric if only that which makes him different is regarded as authentic. The criterion may help us understand where Jesus's teaching is exceptional, but it can never give us the essential Jesus.[5]

Second, the Jesus Seminar is inconsistent in applying the criterion. On the one hand, the Fellows use the criterion when it works to their advantage. They believe John the Baptist did indeed baptize Jesus, because (1) John the Baptist performed the baptism of Jesus himself whereas other Jewish groups, like the Dead Sea Scrolls Community, had the candidates baptize themselves, and (2) the later church was embarrassed by John's baptism of Jesus because it made the latter subservient to the former. But, other times, when the results of the application of the criterion of dissimilarity confirm evangelical convictions about Jesus, the Fellows reject the conclusions. Luke 5:33–35 says that Jesus did not fast. The Seminar argues that although Jesus's action is different from Judaism and early Christianity, both of which practiced fasting, the remark is nevertheless not genuine. Or take the example of the title "Son of Man." While most Gospel scholars accept the title Son of Man as coming from Jesus because (1) it was not a title for the Messiah in the Judaism of Jesus's day and (2) the early church did not use the name "Son of Man" for Jesus, nevertheless the Jesus Seminar rejects it as authentic. It becomes clear in all of this that the Fellows want to have their cake and eat it too. As long as the criterion of dissimilarity supports their liberal bias, it is okay. If it doesn't, they disregard the guideline's application.

115

Truthfully, the criterion of dissimilarity itself can strike the reader as ludicrous because we recognize in ourselves that our words and deeds reflect in some way our culture. How can one possibly arrive at true portraits of individuals by stripping them of their heritage and considering only those acts and deeds as genuine that appear to be entirely dissimilar from their culture? While Jesus certainly was not merely a collection of words and actions reflecting the ethos of his day, and he surely opposed the religious system of the time, he nevertheless lived in the midst and partook of his native Jewish environment.

MULTIPLE ATTESTATION

Multiple attestation occurs when a purported saying or act of Jesus occurs in multiple sources: Mark, Q (the 235 sayings Jesus, Luke, and Matthew share in common), M (Matthew's special material), L (Luke's special material). Here, again, the Fellows used the guideline inconsistently. On the one hand, they believe Jesus's praise of John the Baptist in Matthew 11:7–11 is probably genuine because it is found in Q and in the *Gospel of Thomas*. But on the other hand, though Mark 10:45 ("For even the Son of Man did not come to be served, but to serve, and to give his life as a ransom for many" [NIV]) is similar to Matthew 26:24; Luke 22:19–20; and 1 Corinthians 11:24–25, the Jesus Seminar declares it to be probably inauthentic. This conclusion is all the more lamentable since "Son of Man," as we saw before, meets the criterion of dissimilarity.

But even if this criterion is applied perfectly, it simply fails to convince. Just because it is recorded in only one Gospel, why would that make the saying or action inauthentic? Why does it have to be corroborated to be authentic? Certainly the Gospels are not meant to be simply identical copies of one another.

CONCLUSION

When one learns where the Fellows of the Jesus Seminar are coming from—their heroes, their "seven pillars of scholarly

116

wisdom," and their agenda—it is not difficult to see why they arrived at the color-coded translation of the Gospels. This is not a group of biblical scholars who represent the gamut of theological beliefs but rather a group of people who fit the Gospels into their own left-wing theological perspective, thus going against their own premise that one must not create a portrait of a "Jesus who is congenial to you."

Their methodology is flawed, including the two criteria they use to determine the authentic words and deeds of Jesus and the high status they give to the *Gospel of Thomas*. From their perspective, only Jesus's virtuous life remains as being historically accurate. The rest—Jesus's virgin birth, his vicarious death, victorious resurrection, and visible return—are judged to be mere stories or myths perpetuated by the church. This matter has enormous implications. We do not commit our lives simply to a good, well-intentioned but deluded man. Rather, as Christians, we commit our lives to the risen Christ, to one who is all he claimed to be and one who will one day return to fully establish his kingdom.

The Gnostic Jesus: The Third Quest for the Historical Jesus (1980s to the Present)

The Jesus Seminar basically finished its work about a decade ago, but its emphasis on noncanonical gospels over against the traditional Gospels continues to make its influence today through *The Da Vinci Code* and especially through the most prolific writer on the Gnostic gospels today—Elaine Pagels. If Pagels and her Ivy League colleagues have their way, the *Gospel of Thomas* will replace the four Gospels, especially the Gospel of John. We turn now to her radical spin on Jesus and the kingdom of God.

Elaine Pagels, Harrington Spear Paine Professor of Religion at Princeton University, has long championed the Gnostic cause in American religion. Her bestsellers on the subject include *The Gnostic Gospels*, *The Gnostic Paul*, and *Adam, Eve, and the Serpent.* In her most recent bestseller, *Beyond Belief: The Secret Gospel of Thomas*,[6] Pagels argues that the *Gospel of Thomas* has received a bad rap thanks to the canonical Gospel of John. Her title reflects the thesis of her book: the Gospel of John presents only one part of the story of early Christianity, and not a very legitimate one at that. She asserts that the Gospel of John promotes a religion in which individuals should cognitively believe a set of dogmas about Jesus (that he is the only Son of God, uniquely existing in eternity past, born of the virgin Mary, died for sinful humanity, and arose in bodily form), and anything other than these formulations are to be categorically rejected as heresy. The *Gospel of Thomas*, on the other hand, argues Pagels, presents a more promising path, a religion in which truth is not revelation from God outside the individual but rather truth about God within the individual waiting to be discovered and experienced. The content of that truth is that Christians are actually none other than Christ, newly created in the image of God! Pagels claims vociferously that the Gospel of John was written precisely to quash the growing popularity of *Thomas* in the first-century church.

Authority: Where Does It Come From?

The real question here is where does authority come from? What should be the canon? Should it be the New Testament or the apocryphal, noncanonical gospels of the second to fourth centuries AD? With this question Pagels goes for the jugular of historic Christianity, arguing that Gnosticism was (and is) just as legitimate, if not more so, an expression of Christianity as orthodoxy. Her question basically is, Who made historic Christianity the final say in matters of faith and practice? The key issue behind this question has to do with the New Testament canon—the books that are traditionally included in the New Testament.

Canon means rule or measuring stick. Discussions of the final formation of the Bible center on at least two important questions: When were the books of the Bible determined to be inspired? And what were the criteria for including the present books in the Bible? For our purposes, we will focus only on the New Testament canon. Pagels's thesis is twofold: Before Irenaeus there was diversity of opinion about the nature of Christ, even in the New Testament itself. In other words, the New Testament canon was open. But from Irenaeus on, an artificial uniformity was imposed on Christianity regarding who Jesus was. Consequently, the historical winners (the four Gospels) were officially admitted into the canon, while the historical losers (the *Gospel of Thomas,* for example) were shunned. After summarizing Pagels's arguments below, I will offer a rebuttal of them, point by point.

The Gospel(s) according to Pagels

Pagels wastes no time in her book *Beyond Belief* debunking the idea that there was a uniform witness to the nature of Christ early on in the history of Christianity. In reality, claims Pagels, there were at least three major competing interpretations of who Jesus was at that time, reflected in the Synoptic Gospels, the Gospel of John, and the *Gospel of Thomas.*

THE SYNOPTICS

Pagels wants to pit the Gospel of John against the Synoptic Gospels (Matthew, Mark, and Luke) to support her theory that there were diverse, contradictory views about Christ in the New Testament. Thus she mentions the well-known differences between the Synoptics and John: the Synoptics place Jesus's cleansing of the temple in the passion week, while John situates it at the beginning of Jesus's ministry (John 2:12–22); and the Synoptics equate the Last Supper with the Passover meal, while John does not, for he wishes to equate Jesus's death on the cross with the time of the slaying of the Passover lamb.

Most evangelicals are not threatened by these dissimilarities, attributing them to John's poetic license. But Pagels goes on to insist that the Synoptics' view of the nature of Christ is that, though labeled the "Messiah," the "Son of Man," and "Son of God" therein, Jesus was no more than God's *human* agent! These titles were but metaphors not to be pressed literally. According to Pagels, only Luke's Gospel says that Jesus was made Lord, but only at his resurrection, not before.

THE GOSPEL OF JOHN

According to Pagels, the portrait of Jesus dramatically changes with John, for that Gospel elevates him to equal status with God. It is only in the Gospel of John that Jesus is the unique Son of God, the light of the world, and without parallel among humans. Pagels labels this "higher Christology" (Jesus is God) as opposed to the Synoptics' "lower Christology" (Jesus is mere man).

THE GOSPEL OF THOMAS

The *Gospel of Thomas,* unlike the Gospel of John, teaches that God's light shines not only in Jesus but, potentially at least, in everyone. Thomas's gospel encourages the hearer not so much to believe in Jesus (as John 20:3–31 does), but rather to seek to know God through one's own divinely given capacity, since all are created in the image of God:

> The Kingdom is inside you, and outside you. When you come to know yourselves, then you will be known, and you will see that it is you who are the children of the living Father. But if you will not know yourselves, you dwell in poverty, and it is you who *are* that poverty.
>
> *Gospel of Thomas*, 3

When the would-be followers of Jesus look within themselves, they discover that not only does Jesus come from the light, so do they:

If they say to you, "Where did you come from?" say to them,
"We *came from the light, the place where the light came
into being by itself*, and was revealed through their image."
If they say to you, "Who are you?" say, "We are its children,
the chosen of the living father."

Gospel of Thomas, 50 (author's emphasis)

The *Gospel of Thomas* equates humans with Christ: "Whoever drinks from my mouth will become as I am, and I myself
will become that person, and the mysteries shall be revealed
to him" (108).

Then Pagels asserts: "This, I believe, is the symbolic meaning of attributing this gospel to Thomas, whose name means
'twin.' By encountering the 'living Jesus,' as Thomas suggests,
one may come to recognize oneself and Jesus as, so to speak,
identical twins."[7] Then approvingly she quotes *Thomas* in
that regard:

Since you are my twin and my true companion, examine
yourself, and learn who you are. . . . Since you will be called
my [twin], . . . although you do not understand it yet . . . you
will be called "the one who knows himself." For whoever has
not known himself knows nothing, but whoever has known
himself has simultaneously come to know the depth of all
things.[8]

While Pagels believes that early Christianity offered various
contradictory perspectives on Jesus (the Synoptics, John,
and *Thomas*), she resonates only with the *Thomas* perspective. She bemoans that the complexity and richness of early
Christianity was lost with Irenaeus, second-century bishop
of Lyons, France, who imposed, she believes, an artificial
uniformity onto the church. Irenaeus was an ardent combat-
ant against Gnosticism, prompting his five-volume polemical
work *Refutation and Overthrow of Falsely So-Called Knowledge*, commonly referred to as *Against Heresies*. In those
five volumes, the bishop affirmed the notion of "apostolic

tradition," that is, the orthodox view of Jesus Christ that had been handed down by the apostles to each succeeding generation, namely, his birth from a virgin, his passion and resurrection in the flesh, and all unique revelatory events that provided atonement for sin. As such, Irenaeus asserts that this apostolic tradition represents the canon of truth, the grid through which to filter out false teaching about Jesus.

According to Pagels, Irenaeus was among the first to champion the Gospel of John as the true interpretation of Jesus, linking it to the Synoptics, even interpreting the Synoptics through John's perspective. Consequently, Irenaeus declared that these four Gospels exclusively conveyed the true message about Jesus—that he is the unique Son of God whose sacrificial death alone provides forgiveness of sin. Irenaeus secured such a privileged position for the four Gospels (read through John's perspective) by mounting a campaign against all apocryphal gospels, demanding they be destroyed.[9]

Irenaeus set the church on a path that led to the victory of orthodoxy over alternate expressions of Jesus, culminating in the official approval of the four Gospels and the apostolic tradition by Athanasius, fourth-century champion of orthodoxy. Such a development was aided by the Roman emperor Constantine, whose conversion to Christianity in AD 313 paved the way for the legalizing of Christianity. Using Christianity as the unifying principle for his empire, Constantine convened the bishops of the churches in Nicea, on the Turkish coast, in AD 325 for the purpose of composing a common set of beliefs among Christians—the Nicene Creed. In the spring of AD 367, Bishop Athanasius of Alexandria, Egypt, wrote his most famous letter. In his Easter letter to the churches, Athanasius clarified the picture of Christ that had been sketched out two hundred years before, starting with Irenaeus. First, the bishop censured the heretics. They

have tried to reduce into order for themselves the books termed apocryphal and to mix them up with the divinely inspired Scripture . . . which those who were eyewitnesses and helpers of the Word delivered to the fathers, it seemed good to me . . . *to set forth in order the books included in the canon and handed down and accredited as divine.*[10]

Pagels remarks:

After listing the twenty-two books that he says are "believed to be the Old Testament" [based on the Hebrew reckoning], Athanasius proceeds to offer the earliest known list of the twenty-seven books he called the "books of the New Testament," beginning with "the four Gospels, Matthew, Mark, Luke, and John," and proceeding to the same list of writings attributed to apostles that constitute the New Testament today. Praising these as the "springs of salvation," he calls upon Christians during this Lenten season to "cleanse the church from every defilement" and to reject "the apocryphal books," which are "filled with myths, empty, and polluted"—books that, he warns, "encite conflict and lead people astray."[11]

The Argument against Pagels

Pagels makes essentially two arguments. First, she maintains that, before Irenaeus, diversity characterized not only early Christianity but even the New Testament. Second, she argues that a forced uniformity became the mark of the church's teaching from Irenaeus on. I take issue with those two claims.

THE QUESTION OF DIVERSITY

First, it simply is not true that diversity to the point of contradiction characterizes the Synoptics' relationship to John. Not only does the Gospel of John teach that Jesus is God, but so do the Synoptics. This is clear from the Synoptics' titles for Jesus, contra Pagels: Messiah, Son of Man, and Son of God. *Messiah* is the Hebrew term for "anointed one" (*Christ* is the Greek term for the same). It is clear from

123

Psalm 2:2, 7 that the term does not refer to a mere man, for there the Lord's Anointed One (Messiah in v. 2) is proclaimed the Son of God (v. 7). Even in a Jewish work written close in time to the New Testament, *4 Ezra*, we see God call the Messiah "my son."

A similar dynamic exists for the title "Son of Man," Jesus's favorite self-reference. This title originated in Daniel 7, where it is the *heavenly* Son of Man who receives the kingdom of God (Dan. 7:13–14). "Son of God," as we saw in Psalm 2, elevates the Messiah far above humans. Furthermore, in ancient Egyptian and Mesopotamian thought as well as in the Roman Empire, the pharaoh or king was declared to be the Son of God—one divinely begotten of God. The use of these three titles for Jesus in the Synoptics, then—Messiah, Son of Man, and Son of God—surely demonstrates that they view Jesus as more than a mere man.

Moreover, Pagels asserts that the Gospel of John consciously opposed the *Gospel of Thomas*. She says this because she believes that *Thomas* dates back to around AD 50, although most scholars date *Thomas* in the second century. The proof of this, according to Pagels, is that the *Gospel of Thomas* must have been extant in the first century because John criticizes it and paints such a negative picture of the apostle Thomas. Thus Thomas does not understand that Lazarus will rise from the dead (John 11:14–16); he does not comprehend that Jesus is the way to heaven (14:5–6); and most important, he has to see the risen Jesus before he will believe Jesus is no longer dead (20:24–28). But there is no need to draw the conclusion from these failings of Thomas that John was criticizing a *written* document about Thomas; after all, the first two responses were typical of the misunderstandings of the disciples toward Jesus in general during the life of Christ.

Furthermore, John 20:24–28 serves the purpose of confirming that Jesus arose bodily from the dead, so Thomas was able to see and touch Christ. But the "target" for this passage need not have been the *Gospel of Thomas*, for the beginning forms of Gnosticism in the first century AD denied the bodily resurrection of Jesus, and John 20:24–28 is better suited as a barb against it. Scholars date the beginnings of Gnosticism—but not the full-blown system presumed in *Thomas*—to the late first century AD, with the *Gospel of Thomas* following decades later. If this is so, then Pagels's entire thesis collapses to the ground, for it cannot uphold a first-century dating of the *Gospel of Thomas*. All of this to say, the four canonical Gospels espouse a consistent message about Jesus Christ—though he was fully human, he was fully God.

To summarize, Pagels states that the Synoptics do not agree with John, nor do they agree with the *Gospel of Thomas*. However, the real picture that emerges is that the Synoptics are very similar to John in their portraits of Jesus and together they disagree with the noncanonical *Thomas*'s presentation of Jesus as Gnostic. The bottom line is that it's the noncanonical *Thomas* versus the Synoptics and John.

THE QUESTION OF THE ORIGIN OF ORTHODOXY

Neither will Pagels's second thesis do—that only from Irenaeus on was there a forced uniformity on the church's teaching about Jesus. In other words, she believes Gnostic writings like *Thomas* were held in high regard among Christians, along with the Synoptics and John, until Irenaeus messed things up. But this assumption overlooks a crucial fact: orthodoxy runs throughout the New Testament and is witnessed to consistently up to Irenaeus and far beyond. In the Pastoral Epistles 1 and 2 Timothy and Titus, written circa AD 64, the author (Paul) admonishes pastors Timothy and Titus to preserve and protect the "sound doctrine" (1 Tim. 1:10; 6:3; 2 Tim. 1:13; 4:3; Titus 1:9). This sound teaching is no doubt the teaching of the apostles (Acts 2:42) concerning Jesus's birth, death, and resurrection.

Second Peter (ca. AD 64) vows to protect that same truth (1:1; 2), as does Jude (ca. AD 80), urging the believers to defend "the faith which was once for all delivered to the saints" (v. 3 RSV). Most likely, these biblical authors were combating the beginning expressions of Gnosticism. First John (ca. AD 95) rounds out the discussion by providing a more sustained criticism of Gnostic teaching (1:1; 2:22; 3:4, 8–10; 4:2–3).

This is all in keeping with the message of the Gospel of John that Jesus is the God-man (see especially the opening statement 1:1–14). Irenaeus and Athanasius were not the first to "impose" the canonical rule of faith. In reality, the Church Fathers all the way from Justin Martyr (early second century AD) to Augustine (early fifth century AD) attest to the orthodox belief in Jesus. We see this from the fact that, while the Fathers quote the twenty-seven New Testament books some 36,000 times, in comparison, their references to the New Testament Apocrypha are negligible. They also chose to read and preach on the twenty-seven New Testament books in their worship services.

The necessary conclusion to be drawn from all of this is that it looks very much like orthodox Christianity was far and away the dominant view of early Christianity, beginning from New Testament times and continuing with the Church Fathers all the way to the Council of Nicea in AD 325 and beyond. By way of contrast, Gnosticism and the writings it spawned (the *Gospel of Thomas* and the other fifty apocryphal documents discovered at Nag Hammadi in 1945) were the view of a few extremists whose message the collective church rejected—and rightly so.

THE NEW TESTAMENT CANON

It would be fitting to conclude this discussion of authority by briefly stating what most biblical scholars—minus Pagels and her colleagues—say about the New Testament canon. The answers to the two questions posed near the beginning of this section are as follows.

First, when were the twenty-seven books of the New Testament recognized to be inspired (in other words, from God)? The answer is AD 200. By then the churches were reading and the Church Fathers were preaching from all twenty-seven books that now comprise the New Testament. This prior practice was later confirmed at the Council of Carthage (AD 397). That assembly of church leaders, held in Carthage, North Africa, determined that only canonical works should be read in the churches. Then they listed the twenty-seven books now comprising the New Testament as inspired writings.

The second question was, What were the criteria for including the present books and no more in the New Testament? The Church Fathers applied five criteria:

1. Does it have apostolic authority?
2. Does the writing in question go back to the first century?
3. Does the writing subscribe to orthodoxy?
4. Was the book read in the churches?
5. Did the people of God sense the book was inspired?

The simple result of the application of these tests in the second to the fourth centuries AD was that the books of the New Testament were admitted into the canon, while writings by the Gnostics and others (the *Gospel of Thomas* included) were not. And there is no reason for the modern church to do anything different now. When it comes to the proper view of Jesus, the New Testament is our sole authority—not Gnostic books like the *Gospel of Thomas* that tried unsuccessfully to force themselves on the people of God.

Conclusion

In this chapter we have interacted with skeptical views about Jesus and the kingdom, those who deny that the end-time kingdom of God dawned in the life and ministry of the historical Jesus. The first quest for the historical Jesus presented Jesus as an apocalyptic preacher who wrongly predicted the advent of the kingdom—the millennium—in his lifetime.

While we agreed with Schweitzer that Jesus was an apocalyptic preacher, we also believe he was more than that. Jesus was the Christ, the heavenly Son of Man, the Son of God, in whose sayings and miracles God's kingdom dawned. And the resurrection of Jesus proved this to be so.

I also rejected the second quest for the historical Jesus—the form critic Jesus—on the grounds that the four Gospels are historically reliable because they are divinely inspired. Thus the Jesus of history is none other than the Christ of faith. And the Gnostic Jesus of the third quest for the historical Jesus fared no better in my estimation. It simply stretches credulity to think that the *Gospel of Thomas* should rival the Gospel of John. Nor should any other apocryphal gospel be added to the time-honored works of Matthew, Mark, Luke, and John.

6

Hermeneutics, Prophecy, and Apocalypticism

Making Good Sense of the Millennium

In this last chapter we arrive at the heart of the issue of the millennium and, indeed, the crux of the problem of end-time prophecy: hermeneutics. *Hermeneutics* means interpretation. And the study of hermeneutics and Scripture has a long and distinguished history, beginning in the New Testament and continuing until the present day. When it comes to end-time prophecy and the millennium in particular, one has to engage in a discussion of the biblical genres of prophecy and apocalyptic literature. But before examining these two types of literature in the Bible, as to how we are to interpret them, I begin this chapter by offering my own interpretation of the millennium in light of the previous chapters.

The End of the World as We Know It

My view of the millennium is an eclectic one. Thus, in my view, the preterist interpretation, which recognizes the already aspect of the kingdom of God/millennium has much to commend it. The fall of Jerusalem to the Romans in AD 70 occupies an important place in New Testament prophecy (at least in the first half of the Olivet Discourse and as the backdrop for Revelation). Still, however, as I argued earlier, it doesn't make sense to equate the fall of Jerusalem with Jesus's parousia.

On the other hand, the futurist emphasis on the not-yet aspect of the kingdom and the millennium offers a healthy corrective to the preterist view. The kingdom of God come to earth is still future, which will be established at the second coming of Christ. But in my opinion and as I mentioned before, the futurist school of interpretation does not recognize enough the presence of the kingdom of God today in our world, thanks to the first coming of Christ and the establishment of his church.

Thus we are left with the amillennial/idealist, already/not-yet construct for interpreting the kingdom of God. The kingdom is already here but not yet complete. I believe that there is much truth in this position. Yet this venerable view allegorizes unnecessarily Revelation 20 along the lines of Platonic dualism, which I suspect was foreign to the New Testament authors, John included. That is to say, the premillennial reading of Revelation 20 seems to make much more sense.

In light of all that I have tried to say thus far in this work, I offer the following reading of end-time prophecy and the millennium. First, I'll give my view in chart form, and then I'll explain it in a little more detail.

Reading these Scriptures according to this chart, the already/not-yet eschatological tension pertains more to the *temporary messianic kingdom* (a phenomenon attested to in Jewish apocalyptic writings contemporaneous with the New Testament) than it does to the eternal kingdom of God. If we posit two aspects of the temporary messianic kingdom—Christ's kingdom established at his first coming, which is at war with Satan, and Christ's kingdom that will prevail over Satan at the

An Eclectic View of End-Time Prophecy and the Millennium

The New Testament as a whole, especially Revelation 1–18	Olivet Discourse and Revelation 19	Revelation 20:1–6	Revelation 20:7–15	Revelation 21–22
The temporary kingdom of Christ dawned spiritually at the first coming of Christ	The second coming of Christ at the end of history	Establishment of physical, temporary (one-thousand-year) kingdom of Christ on earth	Temporary rebellion against Christ by Gog-Magog at the end of Christ's one-thousand-year reign	Eternal state/ new heaven and new earth
Already: dawned with the first coming of Christ Not yet: battles with Satan and the messianic woes continuing now	Already: end of messianic woes/ rule of Antichrist	Already: Christ's kingdom rules the earth/Christians rule with him	Not yet: one last rebellion against God's Christ and his people	The eternal kingdom of God

parousia—then we pretty much solve the major interpretive difficulties of Revelation 20 and, for that matter, biblical end-time prophecy as a whole. Thus, on the one hand, we allow for the symbolic nature of prophetic-apocalyptic writings (see below), which allows for the kingdom to be both present and yet at war with Satan in the tribulation period now. And these two concurrent realities—kingdom and tribulation—will intensify until the parousia. And yet on the other hand, we can allow the literal reality behind the symbols of Revelation 20 to stand, namely, a kingdom clearly to be established on the earth in the future. And, as I noted in chapter 2, the model I am proposing—present, temporary messianic kingdom leading to the eternal kingdom of God—was embraced in Jewish literature at the time of the New Testament.

Now I will summarize the interpretation of the genres of prophecy and apocalypticism, two related but different biblical genres.

The Genre of Prophecy

As I noted in chapter 1, predictive prophecy in both the Old and New Testaments can have near and far fulfillments. Often scholars call this near-and-far-fulfillments dynamic "prophetic telescoping," the phenomenon of prophecy leaping from one prominent peak in predictive topography to another, without notice of the valley of time coming between them. For example, many think Psalm 22, Isaiah 53, and Daniel 9 blend the first and second advents of Christ into one coming.

Now I will offer a more general principle of interpretation to account for this prophetic telescoping of near and far fulfillments in the Old Testament. The near fulfillment of a prophet's prediction happened during or not too long after his day (usually with regard to judgment on Israel, though occasionally it envisioned God's temporary deliverance of Israel; for example, see Isaiah 7), but often the far fulfillment pertained to the future restoration of Israel to her land after the Babylonian captivity (587–539 BC). This principle of interpretation is reasonable because the dominant subject matter of the Old Testament prophets had to do with Israel—her idolatry and God's subsequent judgment on her—but also with Israel's repentance and future restoration after the Assyrian (722 BC) and Babylonian invasions (605–587 BC). Thus, for example, Isaiah, Jeremiah, Ezekiel, Daniel, Hosea, Joel, Micah, Habakkuk, and Zechariah all focus on two major predictive prophecies: Israel's defeat at the hands of the Assyrians or Babylonians, respectively (the near fulfillment) and Israel's future restoration to her land after those divine judgments (the far fulfillment). The point to be gleaned from this prophetic telescoping model is that both near and far fulfillments were expected to occur *in* history, not at its end! This is why Old Testament prophecy is more hopeful than apocalyptic literature about the future of the world (see comments to follow).

But something changed the face of Old Testament prophecy dramatically and gave rise to apocalyptic literature; namely, even though Israel returned to her land in 536 BC, subsequent centuries demonstrated that Israel was still in *exile*. After Jews returned to Israel after the Babylonian exile, nation after nation continued to run roughshod over Palestine: Persia, Greece, Egypt, Syria, and Rome. With each successive regime's takeover of Palestine, the realization grew that the long-awaited promise of the restoration of Israel *in* history had not happened. Consequently, the genre of prophecy gave way to the genre of apocalypticism. And in that literature, the far fulfillment *in* history of predictive prophecy was replaced with the expectation of a final fulfillment at the *end* of history, at the end of the world as the ancients knew it. And so it was that Jewish apocalyptic writings emerged and flourished in very difficult times for Jews, especially between 200 BC and AD 100. This period overlapped with the New Testament, which contains its own apocalyptic writings (see below).

We turn now to the genre of apocalyptic literature.[1]

The Genre of Apocalyptic Literature

Jewish and Christian apocalyptic literature usually contains the following items:

1. The work often focuses on a well-known and beloved Old Testament person (like Enoch or Moses) and makes him the hero of the book.
2. This hero often takes a journey, accompanied by a celestial guide who shows him interesting sights and comments on them.
3. Information is often communicated through visions.
4. The visions often make use of strange, even enigmatic, symbolism.

133

5. The visions often are pessimistic with regard to the possibility that human intervention will ameliorate the present situation.

6. The visions usually end with God's bringing the present situation to a cataclysmic end and establishing his kingdom.

7. The apocalyptic writer often uses a pseudonym, claiming to write in the name of his chosen hero.

8. The writer often takes past history and rewrites it as if it were prophecy.

9. The focus of apocalyptic literature is on comforting and sustaining the righteous remnant.[2]

Let us now see the logic behind the above components of apocalyptic literature. First, the literature is *pessimistic* because the minority righteous is being persecuted by the majority unrighteous (numbers 5 and 9 above). Because of this, the righteous hold out no hope for God's deliverance in history; rather, they believe their vindication will come only at the end of history, when humans are no longer in control. Second, apocalyptic literature is *dualistic*, dividing reality into two stages or periods: this age (the kingdom of Satan) and the age to come (the kingdom of God) (see number 6). Third, apocalyptic literature is *futuristic*—the kingdom of God/age to come will arrive at the end of history when the Messiah or God himself will show up to take visible charge of things (implied in number 6). This is in keeping with the very definition of *apocalypse*, which means to "unveil" the future. Fourth, apocalyptic literature is *symbolic* (numbers 2, 3, and 4), for how else could one interpret the end of the world other than by using figurative, dramatic language? Fifth, apocalyptic literature claimed to be *canonic*; that is, it should be considered divinely inspired like the rest of the Old Testament. Thus the anonymous apocalyptic Jewish author wrote under the guise of a recognized Old Testament author (numbers 1 and 7). Moreover, the apocalyptic author turned history into prophecy to give the impression that he had predictive prowess from God. And if he correctly predicted the past, then what he forecast about the future would surely come to pass as well!

With the exceptions of numbers 7 and 8, conservative Christian scholars feel comfortable with applying the preceding apocalyptic features to the New Testament: the Olivet Discourse; 1 Thessalonians 4; 2 Thessalonians 2; 2 Peter 3; and especially Revelation.

See the following chart and comments that follow for a summary of the distinction between prophecy and apocalyptic literature.

Predictions

Old Testament	*Already/Near Fulfillment* *In* history; for example, Isaiah 1–39—Babylonian judgment on Israel	*Not-Yet/Far Fulfillment* *In* history; for example, Isaiah 40–66—Israel's restoration to her land
Intertestamental Judaism (200 BC–AD 100)	*Already/Near Fulfillment* *In* history: prophecy; for example, Daniel 9:24–27—Maccabean Revolt against Antiochus Epiphanes	*Not-Yet/Far Fulfillment* At *end* of history: apocalyptic; for example, Daniel 9:24–27—Antichrist at end of history
New Testament	*Already/Near Fulfillment* *In* history: prophecy; for example, first half of Olivet Discourse—fall of Jerusalem in AD 70	*Not-Yet/Far Fulfillment* At *end* of history: apocalyptic; for example, second half of Olivet Discourse—parousia of Christ

- In the Old Testament, Isaiah illustrates prophecy at its finest. Isaiah 1–39 predicts that God will soon judge Israel for her idolatry and injustice by sending her away into Babylonian captivity, which indeed happened in 587 BC. But Isaiah 40–66 envisions a future, glorious return of Israel to her land to defeat the enemies of God, which was thought to happen in 536 BC.

135

- In the intertestamental period, the time between the Old Testament and the New Testament, Daniel represents classic apocalyptic literature. Daniel 9:24–27 deals with the reinterpretation of the prophecy of Jeremiah that the seventy years of Babylonian exile will be over soon and Israel will be able to return to her land. This is reinterpreted in the prediction in Daniel 9:24–27, which lengthens the 70 years into 70 times 7 years, or 490 years. While the near fulfillment of the 490 years occurred in the Jewish revolt against Antiochus Epiphanes, the cruel Syrian ruler who invaded Palestine in 171 BC, the far fulfillment is thought by many to await the rise of the Antichrist at the *end* of history. So we might say that the near fulfillment/the already of Daniel 9:24–27 in the Maccabean period (167 BC) is biblical prophecy, while the far fulfillment/the not yet at the end of history is apocalyptic in orientation.

- The Olivet Discourse follows a similar pattern: the near fulfillment/already prophecy in the first half of the discourse refers to the fall of Jerusalem to Rome in AD 70; the far fulfillment/not-yet apocalyptic section in the second half of the discourse refers to the second coming of Christ at the end of history.

These comments about the genres of prophecy and apocalyptic literature can be applied to my eclectic view of the millennium in the following self-explanatory chart:

First Coming of Christ	*Near fulfillment* of temporary messianic kingdom on earth but at war with Satan	*Already aspect* • prophecy • in history
Second Coming of Christ	*Far fulfillment* of temporary messianic kingdom/millennium —triumph on earth over Satan	*Not-yet aspect* • apocalyptic • end of history

Conclusion

Having offered my own eclectic interpretation of the millennium and end-time events and my perspective on how we might best understand prophecy, apocalyptic literature, and the relationship between them, I offer here a list of Jewish and Christian apocalyptic literature with the dates of their writing (though these dates are debated).

Daniel (550 BC)

Ezekiel 38–39 (550 BC)

Zechariah 9–14 (500 BC)

1 Enoch (150 BC)

Jubilees (150 BC)

Psalms of Solomon (50 BC)

Assumption of Moses (50 BC)

2 Thessalonians 2 (AD 55)

Mark 13—Matthew 24; Luke 21 (AD 60–70)

Apocalypse of Moses (AD 70)

Sibylline Oracles (AD 80)

4 Ezra (AD 90)

2 Baruch (AD 90)

Revelation (AD 95)

The list of biblical prophetic writings would include the other Old Testament prophets not mentioned above as well as the New Testament, minus the apocalyptic literature above.

Perhaps it is in the combination of prophecy and apocalyptic literature that we find the right balance in handling "end-time" events in the Bible. Thus prophecy reminds us that God is at work establishing his kingdom in the world through his people *in history*. But lest we labor under the false assumption humans can bring on the kingdom of God and adopt the perspective of the social gospel or the skeptics of the Gospels, the apocalyptic mind-set in Scripture reminds us that such a kingdom ultimately awaits the end of history when only Christ himself will make all things right at his return.

Conclusion

The Practicalities of Prophecy

This concluding chapter will ponder how biblical prophecy should impact our lives today.[1] What we have been describing in this volume is the theological mind-set of the already/ not-yet end-time tension that exists between the first and second comings of Christ. And it is to the New Testament that we must ultimately look to answer the question of how we are to respond to Christ's imminent return. As we do, I believe five key responses of the first-century church emerge that together serve as a model for Christians to emulate in the twenty-first century.

Evangelism

In response to the imminent return of Christ, *the early church became heavily engaged in evangelism.* The two ideas—the second coming of Christ and evangelism—are complementary; after all, one of the signs of the times of Christ's return is his promise that "the gospel must first be preached to all nations" (Mark 13:10; see also Matt. 24:14; Luke 21:12–15). Two texts in particular emphasize the early church's commitment to evangelism in light of the parousia. Like all the passages I will summarize here, these two texts display the already/not-yet eschatological tension. Simply put, the church is to help convert sinners to the spiritual kingdom of God until the physical kingdom arrives.

The first passage I call attention to is the text of the Great Commission in Matthew 28:18–20. According to these verses, the risen Jesus currently possesses all authority in heaven and on earth. This is nothing less than the inauguration of the messianic kingdom and the age to come (see also 1 Cor. 15:20–28; Eph. 1:18–23; Col. 1:13–14), and it points to the already aspect of end-time prophecy. Because King Jesus reigns, sinners are to be converted into his kingdom by faith. Nevertheless, this spiritual reign exists in the context of this present age, as indicated by the words at the end of the Matthew passage: "And surely I am with you always, to the very *end of the age*" (emphasis added). The continuance of the present age refers to the not-yet aspect of end-time prophecy.

Acts 1:3–8 makes basically the same point. The already aspect of the kingdom of God is highlighted in verse 3. There Luke indicates that Jesus's resurrection was, in effect, the beginning of the dawning of the kingdom of God (see 1 Cor. 15:20–25). According to verses 4–5 and 8, the indwelling of God's people by the Holy Spirit (itself a sign of the arrival of the last days; see, for example, Ezek. 36:26–28 and Joel 2:28–29) was confirmation that the kingdom of God had come. According to Acts 1:6–7, however, the apostles mistook Jesus's words to mean that the physical kingdom, including the restoration of Israel, was at hand, a notion the Lord quickly corrected. This is the not-yet aspect of end-time prophecy. Interestingly enough, the task to be discharged between Jesus's first and second comings is worldwide evangelization, through the power of the Spirit (v. 8).

Holy Lifestyle

In looking for the return of Christ, *the early church committed itself to a holy lifestyle*. Many New Testament passages, of which Titus 2:11–14 is a good example, make the point that the proper response to the parousia is to live a godly life. In Titus 2:12 Paul presents the two types of lifestyles that confront people in this present age: ungodliness and righteousness. This tradition of the "two ways" is highlighted in the Old Testament (Gen. 6:5; 8:21; Deuteronomy 8; Psalm 1) and appropriated in the New Testament (Matt. 7:24–29; Gal. 5:16–26; Col. 3:8–14; James 3:13–18). The assumption underlying this teaching is that the children of God will distinguish themselves as a holy people in the midst of this age, which is given over to sin. According to Titus 2:11, 13–14, the age to come has broken into this present age through Jesus's death and resurrection. In other words, the age to come has already dawned but it is not yet complete. The former aspect is attested to in verses 11 and 14, which speak of the appearing, or epiphany, of the grace of God through Christ's death, together with the salvation that he brought (v. 11), and of Christ giving himself for us that he might redeem us (v. 14). The latter aspect is emphasized in verse 13: "We wait for the blessed hope—the glorious appearing [epiphany] of our great God and Savior, Jesus Christ."

The end-time tension that results from the first and second comings of Christ forms the basis for the ethical struggle between the two ways delineated in verse 12. Christians are called to declare their allegiance to the righteousness of the age to come instead of to the ungodliness that characterizes this age. That is, they must live like the people of the age to come while residing in the midst of this present evil age.

141

Indomitable Attitude toward Suffering

The early church displayed an indomitable attitude in the midst of affliction, knowing that suffering produces eternal glory. In fact the early believers recognized that such heavenly glory had already dawned in their hearts by virtue of the resurrection of Jesus but that their bodies would not be transformed until the parousia. Typical of this conviction are passages like Romans 8:17–25; 1 Peter 1:5–9; and Revelation 1:5–9. The attitude informing these passages is rooted in the Jewish apocalyptic belief that righteous suffering in this age ensures heavenly glory in the age to come (see 4 *Ezra* 4:27; 7:12; 2 *Bar.* 15:8; 48:50; *The Damascus Rule* 3:18–20/4:13, 17–18).

The Jewish perspective of the two ages, however, was consecutive in nature—when the Messiah comes, this age will completely give way to the age to come. But according to the New Testament, those two ages now overlap because of the death and resurrection of Christ. Consequently, Christians, because they are in Jesus Messiah, currently and simultaneously participate in the sufferings of Christ's cross and in the glory of his resurrection. But at present this glory characterizes the believer's inner person; not until the parousia will it transform his or her body. This is the basic point made in Romans 8:17–25; 1 Peter 1:5–9; and Revelation 1:5–9.

It may even be that the New Testament understood these afflictions to be the long-awaited messianic woes that were expected to intensify and, like the pains of childbirth, give birth to the Messiah and his glorious reign on earth (see Dan. 12:1; 4 *Ezra* 7:37; 2 *Bar.* 55:6). I noted in chapter 4 that some authors make a rather convincing case for seeing Jesus's suffering on the cross as imprinted by this concept of the messianic woes. And although Jesus has risen to glory, his followers live in between the two ages, hence their simultaneous suffering and glory. One day, however, affliction will completely give way to glory. Indeed, the very presence of such affliction assures the Christian of that future glory.

Discernment

In awaiting the return of Christ, *the early church was not deceived by false teachers*. This discerning attitude was also informed by the already/not-yet tension. On the one hand, the early church recognized that the spirit of the Antichrist had already dawned, especially in those who denied Jesus Christ (see 1 John 2:18–23; cf. John 13:27; 2 Thess. 2:1–12; 1 Tim. 4:1–14; 2 Tim. 4:1–5; 2 Peter 2:1–22; Jude 4–16; Revelation 6–19). On the other hand, Jesus had earlier warned his disciples not to be tricked by such people into thinking that history was necessarily about to culminate (Matt. 24:5–8). Luke 21:8–9 is interesting in this regard, for it makes the point that the spirit of the Antichrist (which basically amounted to people falsely claiming to be the Messiah) was only the *beginning* of the appearance of the signs of the times, not the end. Apparently we are to learn from this statement the fact that there were false teachers in the New Testament era claiming that the end of the world was near. Such people, say the Gospels, are to be avoided.

The church of the twenty-first century can profit from Jesus's warning not to assume that the presence of false teachers (the spirit of the Antichrist) inevitably signals the immediate revelation of the Antichrist. Unfortunately, Christians have a long track record of identifying prominent individuals as the Antichrist: several popes, Adolf Hitler, Benito Mussolini, John F. Kennedy, Henry Kissinger, Mikhail Gorbachev, and Juan Carlos, for example. The same can be said of the enigmatic number 666, which has been equated with everything from credit cards to computers to the hand stamp at Disney World. The modern church needs to do away with such inappropriate speculation, which is informed by an anachronistic reading of current events back into the Bible. When God permits the real Antichrist to be revealed, no one will need to guess his identity, according to 2 Thessalonians 2:1–12. In the meantime, the believer is to be wary of, but not unduly alarmed by, false teachers in regard to the return of Christ.

Continued Submission to the Lordship of Christ

In hoping for the parousia, *the early church was encouraged in its struggle against Satan.* At the cross and resurrection of Christ, the defeat of Satan and his demonic host was secured. At the second coming of Christ, their defeat will be sealed. A number of New Testament passages deal with this tension, including Colossians 2:15. This verse, along with 2:8 and 20, is the classic Pauline text on the defeat of the anti-God spiritual rulers and authorities. Together they illustrate that the cross and resurrection of Christ are bringing about the demise of the evil powers, though their ultimate destruction is yet future. Thus verse 15 portrays the already side of the victory over the principalities, while verses 8 and 20 (the elements of the world, as some interpretations call them) present the not-yet aspect (the demonic figures are still forces to be reckoned with). In verse 15 Christ is said to have triumphed over these angelic powers. The latter description is especially engaging because it calls to mind the ancient Roman triumphal procession, in which the victorious general marched proudly through the streets of Rome to celebrate his military accomplishments over his enemies. Paul applies this imagery to the Christian's spiritual victory over Satan.

But that these spiritual powers have not yet been annihilated, or even domesticated, however, is clear from verses 8 and 20, for there Paul challenges the Colossian Christians not to permit themselves to be enslaved to "the principles of this world," which undoubtedly involve hostile angelic beings. Rather, they need to reaffirm the defeat of the supernatural powers by continually submitting themselves to the lordship of Christ. Such an admonition assumes the not-yet aspect of Paul's perspective on the Christian life.

Conclusion

While there may be more responses of the New Testament church to the imminent return of Christ that could be identified, these five should sufficiently occupy Christians of all times until that event transpires. I wish to conclude my comments on the subject with Paul's word in 1 Thessalonians 4:18. After describing the return of the Lord, the apostle writes: "Therefore encourage each other with these words."

We have seen that biblical prophecy can be misused in a number of ways. Some treat it like a game, playing with prophetic symbols and numbers. Others use prophecy as if it were a weapon, fighting anyone who does not see future things quite the way they do. According to Paul, however, the purpose of biblical prophecy is to comfort and encourage believers. We are confident that Christ will come again to right all the injustices we see in the world and to take us home to be with him forever. We cannot know the exact time of Christ's return, but we must live as if it could happen at any moment. It is this message that empowers Christians to live in the light of the second coming every day of their lives. And it is this message that makes sense of the end of the world as we know it.

Notes

Chapter 1 A Brief History of Prophecy

1. Described in more detail in Russell Chandler, *Doomsday: The End of the World, a View through Time* (Ann Arbor, MI: Servant, 1993), 47–48.

2. Quoted from J. Barton Payne, *Encyclopedia of Biblical Prophecy* (Grand Rapids: Baker, 1980), 681–82.

3. The following comments come from class notes by C. Marvin Pate.

4. This discussion of the kingdom of God is a digest of my article "Kingdom of God" in *Baker Dictionary of Biblical Theology* (Grand Rapids: Baker, forthcoming).

5. The following section draws on Robert G. Clouse, Robert N. Hosack, and Richard V. Pierard, *The New Millennium Manual: A Once and Future Guide* (Grand Rapids: Baker, 1999), chap. 3.

6. "Justin Martyr Dialogue with Trypho, a Jew," in *The Ante-Nicene Fathers: Translation of the Fathers Down to A.D. 325*, ed. A. Roberts and J. Donaldson (Grand Rapids: Eerdmans, 1975), 2:201.

7. For an excellent discussion of these three individuals, see Clouse, Hosack, and Pierard, *New Millennium Manual*, 79–81.

8. Ibid., 79–80.

9. Ibid., 81–82.

10. See ibid., 90.

11. Ibid., 91.

Chapter 2 Thy Kingdom Come

1. Stanley J. Grenz, *The Millennial Maze: Sorting Out Evangelical Options* (Downers Grove, IL: InterVarsity, 1992), 185.

2. J. R. R. Tolkien, *The Return of the King: Being the Third Part of the Lord of the Rings* (Boston: Houghton Mifflin, 1981), 227.

3. C. I. Scofield, *Scofield Reference Bible* (New York: Oxford University Press, 1917), 5, note 4.

4. Ibid., 60.

5. "Historic" in the sense that this perspective can be traced all the way back to the church fathers.

6. See Gleason L. Archer Jr., Paul D. Feinberg, Douglas J. Moo, and Richard R. Reiter, *The Rapture: Pre-, Mid-, or Post-Tribulational?* (Grand Rapids: Zondervan, 1984), 194.

7. This discussion is based on J. Daniel Hays, J. Scott Duvall, and C. Marvin Pate, *Dictionary of Biblical Prophecy* (Grand Rapids: Zondervan, 2007), 341–43.

8. See ibid., 421–22.

Chapter 3 Thy Kingdom Came

1. Craig A. Blaising, Kenneth L. Gentry Jr., and Robert B. Strimple, *Three Views on the Millennium and Beyond*, ed. Darrell L. Bock (Grand Rapids: Zondervan, 1999), 13–14.

2. Paul N. Benware, *Understanding End Times Prophecy: A Comprehensive Approach* (Chicago: Moody, 2006), 120–22.

3. Walter Rauschenbusch, *A Theology for the Social Gospel* (Nashville: Abingdon, 1978), 134. See the helpful summary of Rauschenbusch's theology in Steve Wilkens and Alan G. Padgett, *Christianity and Western Thought: A History of Philosophers, Ideas, and Movements* (Downers Grove, IL: InterVarsity, 2000), 286–88.

4. Rauschenbusch, *Theology for the Social Gospel*, 146.

5. Ibid., 243, 148.

6. Grenz, *Millennial Maze*, 66.

7. Blaising, Gentry, and Strimple, *Three Views on the Millennium and Beyond*, 19.

8. Those taking the biblical postmillennialism view include David Chilton, *The Days of Vengeance: An Exposition of the Book of Revelation* (Fort Worth: Dominion, 1987); and Gary DeMar, *Last Days Madness: Obsession of the Modern Church* (Atlanta: American Vision, 1994).

9. Kenneth L. Gentry Jr., *Before Jerusalem Fell: Dating the Book of Revelation* (Tyler, TX: Institute for Christian Economics, 1989), 15–16.

10. See, for example, Gentry's summary of Revelation 20 from this perspective in *Three Views on the Millennium and Beyond*, 50–55.

11. This point and 6 and 7 that follow come from C. Marvin Pate, ed., *Four Views on the Book of Revelation* (Grand Rapids: Zondervan, 1998), 167–70.

Chapter 4 Thy Kingdom Came/Thy Kingdom Come

1. Other approaches to one degree or another espouse this view: historic premillennialism, progressive dispensationalism, postmillennialism. But still, amillennialism is the most noted proponent of the already/not-yet perspective.

2. Grenz, *Millennial Maze*, 187.

3. See Grenz's comments on this possibility in ibid., 113.

4. It needs to be said here that dispensationalists since the 1960s have rejected the earlier held two-ways approach to salvation, claiming instead that the Old Testament also teaches salvation is by faith and not by the law of Moses.

5. Dale C. Allison Jr., "Eschatology," in *Dictionary of Jesus and the Gospels,* ed. Joel B. Green, Scot McKnight, and I. Howard Marshall (Downers Grove, IL: InterVarsity Press, 1992), 206–8.

6. Raymond Brown, *The Gospel According to John XIII–XXI* (New Haven, CT: Yale University Press, 1970).

7. Raymond Calkins, *The Social Message of Revelation* (New York: Woman's Press, 1920), 3.

8. The Jewish philosopher-theologian Philo (ca. 40 BC) was a notable exception to this rule. Philo interpreted the Old Testament allegorically, which was rooted in his infatuation with Platonic thinking. For documentation on this point and on the point above that most ancient Jews interpreted their Old Testament literally, see Richard Longenecker, *Biblical Exegesis in the Apostolic Period* (Grand Rapids: Eerdmans, 1975), chap. 1.

9. One immediately thinks here of the various works of Karl Barth, C. E. B. Cranfield, James Dunn, and David E. Aune.

Chapter 5 Thy Kingdom Did *Not* Come

1. The following sections on the Jesus Seminar come from C. Marvin and Sheryl Pate, *Crucified in the Media: Finding the Real Jesus amidst Today's Headlines* (Grand Rapids: Baker, 2005), chap. 1; used by permission.

2. The two volumes produced by the Jesus Seminar are *The Five Gospels: What Did Jesus Really Say? The Search for the Authentic Words of Jesus* (San Francisco: HarperSanFrancisco, 1997); and *The Acts of Jesus: What Did Jesus Really Do? The Search for the Authentic Deeds of Jesus* (San Francisco: Harper-SanFrancisco, 1998).

3. Craig L. Blomberg. "Where Do We Start Studying Jesus," in *Jesus under Fire*, ed. Michael J. Wilkins and J. P. Moreland (Grand Rapids: Zondervan, 1995), 18.

4. Unless otherwise specified, the quoted translations of the *Gospel of Thomas* in this chapter come from Wilhelm Schneemelcher, ed., *New Testament Apocrypha*, trans. R. McLain Wilson, vol. 1 of *Gospels and Related Writings* (Cambridge, England: James Clarke; Louisville: John Knox, 1991).

5. Darrell L. Bock, "The Words of Jesus in the Gospels: Live, Jive, or Memorex?" in *Jesus under Fire*, ed. Michael J. Wilkins and J. P. Moreland (Grand Rapids: Zondervan, 1995), 91.

6. Elaine Pagels, *Beyond Belief: The Secret Gospel of Thomas* (New York: Random House, 2003).

7. Ibid., 57.

8. *Gospel of Thomas,* 138, quoted in ibid., 57.

9. Ibid., 80–81, 86, 89–99, 111–13, 147, 166, 167.

10. Athanasius, *Festal Letter* 39.3 (AD 367), author's emphasis.

11. Pagels, *Beyond Belief*, 176–77.

Chapter 6 Hermeneutics, Prophecy, and Apocalypticism

1. N. T. Wright's numerous works make the point essentially that Israel came to realize, even though she had returned to her land, she was still in exile; see, for example, *The New Testament and the People of God* (Minneapolis: Fortress, 1992); and *Jesus and the Victory of God* (Minneapolis: Fortress, 1996).

2. Leon Morris, quoted in Henry A. Virkler, *Hermeneutics: Principles and Processes of Biblical Interpretation* (Grand Rapids: Baker, 1988), 192.

Conclusion

1. This conclusion comes from my *Doomsday Delusions* (Downers Grove, IL: InterVarsity, 1995), 148–55.

C. Marvin Pate is chair of the department of Christian theology and Elma Cobb Professor of Christian Theology at Ouachita Baptist University. He's the author, coauthor, or editor of over fifteen books, including *Doomsday Delusions*, *Reading Revelation*, *Dictionary of Biblical Prophecy and End Times*, and *The End of the Age Has Come*.